CW00951131

THE VELVET COUP

THE VELVET COUP

The Constitution,
the Supreme Court,
and the
Decline of American Democracy

◆

DANIEL LAZARE

VERSO

London • New York

First published by Verso 2001
© Daniel Lazare 2001
All rights reserved

The moral rights of the author have been asserted

Verso
UK: 6 Meard Street, London W1F 0EG
US: 180 Varick Street, New York, NY 10014–4606
www.versobooks.com

Verso is the imprint of New Left Books

ISBN 1–85984–633–5

British Library Cataloguing in Publication Data
A catalogue record is available from the British Library

Library of Congress Cataloging-in-Publication Data
A catalog record for this book is available from the Library of Congress

Typeset in Garamond by Helen Skelton, Brighton, UK
Printed and bound by RR Donnelley & Sons

For Anne

CONTENTS

1

THE COLLAPSE

"IN OR ABOUT December 1910," wrote Virginia Woolf, "human nature changed." Close to a century later, we can be considerably more precise as to when American politics underwent a similar transformation. It was at 2:30 in the morning, Central Standard Time, on November 8, 2000, as Democratic presidential candidate Al Gore's motorcade was pulling into War Memorial Plaza in downtown Nashville. There, before TV cameras, reporters, and exhausted supporters, the vice president was expected to deliver the usual graceful exit speech conceding that his Republican opponent, Texas governor George W. Bush, had eked out a win in the Electoral College despite trailing in the popular vote. Under time-honored rules governing the election of every US president since George Washington, Bush would soon take over the White House.

But then, farther back in the motorcade, an aide's Skytel pager began to vibrate. It was a message from a top Gore strategist back at campaign headquarters named Michael Whouley, whose job that night was to monitor the Florida results. Not so fast, Whouley advised. Where Bush had previously been ahead by 50,000 votes, the latest returns had cut his lead to just 6,000. With a number of precincts as yet uncounted, Florida's twenty-five electoral votes were back in play. Forty-five minutes earlier, Gore had called Bush in Austin to let him know that a formal concession was imminent. Now he picked up the phone to say the opposite.

"Circumstances have changed dramatically since I first called you," he told his opponent. "The state of Florida is too close to call."

"Are you saying what I think you're saying?" replied a stunned George W. "Let me make sure that I understand. You're calling back to retract that concession?"

"Don't get snippy about it!" Gore shot back according to an account pieced together by the *Washington Post.* If Bush prevailed in the final count, he would offer his full support. "But I don't think we should be going out making statements with the state of Florida still in the balance." When Bush protested that his brother, Florida governor Jeb Bush, had personally assured him that the Sunshine State was all locked up, Gore replied that he didn't believe that Jeb was the controlling legal authority in such matters.[1]

Everyone knows, supposedly, what happened next. If Jeb was not the controlling legal authority, then no one was. Over the next few days, Americans watched in astonishment as a country judge in Tallahassee, the Florida Supreme Court, the Florida state legislature, and then the US Supreme Court wrestled over what to do with some 14,000 votes in three counties that were still in dispute. It was monumental foul-up, all the pundits agreed, the equivalent of a four-car head-on collision at a four-way stop sign. Yet no single person or thing was to blame. With the popular vote a dead heat, the Florida tally was crucial. Yet because of an unusual number of election day glitches having to do with butterfly ballots, hanging chads, and whatnot, the Florida tally was indeterminate. The entire political system seemed frozen as a consequence. Newspapers printed detailed accounts of how a similar deadlock between Rutherford B. Hayes and Samuel J. Tilden had caused the 1876 presidential election to wind up in Congress. Yet doomsday forecasters pointed out that this time things could be even messier since, thanks to a constitutional quirk, the House would be in Republican hands as of January 1 while the Senate would be in Democratic. Who would the next president be as of January 20? No one could say. Perhaps Bill Clinton would agree to stay on in the interim. Perhaps, suggested the wits at *Saturday Night Live*, Bush and Gore would agree to share the Oval Office like Oscar and Felix in *The Odd Couple*. Late-night comics had a field day.

But then came the Supreme Court's infamous December 12 ruling, at which point the laughter stopped. The ruling, an unsigned mass of contradictions and absurdities, left court watchers aghast. After halting the Florida recount several days earlier, "The Supremes" had then decided to terminate it altogether on the grounds that the vote counting process had run out of time thanks to a deadline imposed by the Florida state legislature, which had never wanted a recount in the first place. Such reasoning was transparently partisan. Clearly, Republican justices had awarded victory to a Republican candidate so as to insure that control of the court would remain in Republican hands. Yet the Democrats were powerless to do anything about it. The Supreme Court was the highest authority in the land; there was no one left to appeal to. The only comfort they could find was in the thought that, after stealing the presidency in 2000, Republicans would no doubt get their comeuppance in the next round of congressional elections and certainly in the presidential election in 2004. Once voters had given the Republicans what they had coming to them, the Democrats would take back what was rightfully theirs, the electoral process would get back on track, and American democracy would resume its normal course of onward and ever upward.

Having triumphed once again, the republic would emerge "more perfect" by virtue of having survived another test.

THIS IS THE OFFICIAL VERSION, one that sees the events of November–December 2000 as *sui generis* and therefore unreflective of the true state of American democracy. Butterfly ballots, hanging chads, the November 22 "bourgeois riot" aimed at cutting short the Miami recount—the combination was a million-to-one event that was unlikely to ever occur again. Yet the official version is flawed. Narrow as it might have seemed in the wee hours of November 8, Gore's lead in the popular vote was not razor thin. To the contrary, by the time all the absentee ballots had been counted, it had grown to a healthy 540,000 votes, a margin of victory greater than Richard M. Nixon's in 1968 and five times that of John F. Kennedy in 1960. The results in Florida were also not the photo finish that they were portrayed as being. Had all the ballots there been accurately and honestly counted, a statistical analysis by the *Miami Herald* found that Gore would have carried the state by some 23,000 votes.[2] Proportionally, this was a bit less than his lead nationally, 0.38 percent versus 0.5. But it was still hardly microscopic.

Indeed, in international terms, it was hard to know what all the fuss was about. In parliamentary democracies, election officials engage in far finer calibrations in distributing legislative seats according to each party's share of the national vote. When a handful of votes can determine whether a party gains a toehold in the national assembly or is shut out, the allowable margin of error is much less. Yet if Poland and the Czech Republic can accurately tabulate the results for a dozen or more parties at a time, why did the American system have such inordinate trouble tabulating them for just two? If the honesty of election officials in those countries is rarely called into question, why were the results in Florida so dubious that the two parties were immediately at each other's throat?

The answer is that the great unraveling that began on November 7 was not a fluke, but a breakdown of systemic proportions. The problems that the American electoral apparatus faced were ones that any competent system should have been able to handle. Yet, as the pressure mounted, the machinery froze. Thanks to a variety of factors—lackluster candidates, content-less campaigns, a tuned-out electorate, both sides' use of super-sophisticated marketing techniques that were increasingly canceling each other out—election results might reasonably have been expected to be growing narrower rather than broader. This would suggest that the country would need a more finely tuned tallying system. Yet thanks to aging voting machines, ill-trained and ill-paid election workers, and a hyper-fragmented political structure resulting in literally tens of thousands of state and local contests being decided on the same day, the US was winding up with one that was less accurate rather than more. The Electoral College, unchanged since the eighteenth century, added yet another layer of uncertainty. In a pool of 100 million voters, glitches and counting errors could be expected to offset one another to a degree and "wash out" of the final tally. But by dividing the presidential race into fifty smaller state contests, the Electoral College multiplied the chances that an individual mishap could end up having serious reverberations. Rather than reducing the opportunities for failure, it expanded them. As a consequence, the election chaos that erupted in three or four Florida counties was enough to put the state race in doubt and hence the entire national election.

But this was not all. Once the dispute wound up in the hands of the state legislature and the courts, the system froze up again. At the very least, the United States should have had some national election agency capable of taking charge of the process and sorting things out. In India, to cite just one example, an all-powerful election commission sets the dates for elections, arranges for security at thousands of polling places, distributes the ballots, and then takes responsibility for gathering and counting them up—no small task in a country of more 600 million voters, sixteen major language groups, and a dozen-and-a-half major parties. Yet because the authors of the US Constitution had made no such provision back in 1787, Americans two centuries later were at a loss over what to do. As former White House counsel Lloyd Cutler cracked a bit irreverently: "The boys in the powdered wigs didn't get this one right. They didn't anticipate anything like this ever happening, so we find ourselves in a kind of political wilderness"[3]—a wilderness, one might add, from which Americans were unable to find their way out. Indeed, the more judges, local election commissioners, and state legislators tried to intervene, the more the general level of anger and confusion rose. Ultimately, it was left to a former *New York Times* executive editor named Max Frankel to argue on the *Times* op-ed page that although the outcome was "ugly, unfair, confusing or wrong," things might have been worse: there could have been blood in the streets.[4] But the words rang hollow. Rather than settling the dispute peacefully and democratically, the American political system had compounded the problem in such a way as to bring the nation to the brink of an explosion. The only way the system could re-establish control was through a thinly veiled judicial coup d'état—which, of course, was no solution at all.

"The US may be the most technologically advanced country, but our electoral system is any day better," observed M.S. Gill, India's chief election commissioner, on the heels of the Florida fiasco.[5] But, then, scores of other electoral systems around the globe are better as well. As a joke making the rounds of the Third World had it, perhaps next time it would be up to Haiti (or Russia, Serbia, Mozambique, etc.) to send observers to the United States to see to it that the governor of Florida did not again steal the election on his brother's behalf. In parts of the world where the natives are used to hanging their heads in shame whenever Jimmy Carter or Madeleine Albright lectures them on their democratic shortcomings, the schadenfreude was running at high tide.

BUT IF AMERICA'S PERFORMANCE was astonishing on one level, it was quite un-astonishing on another. Mechanisms like the Electoral College, which give state and local officials enormous leeway in determining how elections are to be conducted, date from the late eighteenth century when the infant United States consisted of scattered farms, plantations, and homesteads interspersed with a few coastal cities. It was a decentralized electoral system befitting a decentralized, homespun republic. But two centuries later, America is anything but decentralized. Thanks to round-the-clock cable newscasts, instant polling, and the Internet, information no longer takes weeks to travel by coach or schooner. Instead, it takes just nanoseconds to flash from coast to coast. Such a society needs election methods suitable for a new age, yet as of the year 2000 it was still making do with the same old mechanisms. The results were like traveling on a two-century-old stagecoach between Trenton and Philadelphia. The wonder was not that it took so long, but that the contraption made it at all.

The world's greatest democracy as a teetering old stagecoach— surely there is some mistake? Yet while the United States persists in thinking about itself as the newest of the new, it is in fact the oldest of the old, a polity dating from the days of the French monarchy, the

Venetian republic, and the Holy Roman Empire. All those entities
have long since vanished, yet the US constitutional system staggers on.
In other countries, mechanisms of government are viewed in modern
terms as no less fallible than the beings who made them. They are
machines that must be repaired, updated, and revamped from time to
time in order to remain in good working order. Despite its reputation
for practicality, though, the attitude in the US is almost defiantly pre-
modern. Rather than people like ourselves, the constitutional system,
Americans persist in believing, was made by a race of giants that was
infinitely superior. As no less a constitutional authority than Bill
Clinton observed in mid-November, "Our Founders may not have
foreseen every challenge in the march of democracy, but they crafted a
Constitution that would"—this at a time when the constitutional
system was verging on a nervous breakdown. Yet because the system
was deemed to be superhuman, Americans were no more inclined to
tamper with it than to tamper with, say, the *Mona Lisa*. On those
rare occasions when they did approach the sacred temple and offer
some modestly worded constitutional amendment, they did so only
according to rules established by the Constitution itself, thereby
underscoring their subservience.

Americans see their Constitution as something akin to "the ark of
the covenant, too sacred to be touched," as Jefferson once observed.[6]
The flipside of religious veneration, however, is a feeling of passive
helplessness whenever the machinery goes awry. Rather than making
the necessary repairs, the only thing Americans feel they can do under
such circumstances is cross themselves and hope the machinery will
somehow fix itself. As Kay Bailey Hutchison, a Republican Senator
from Texas, observed following the Supreme Court's velvet coup:
"Now is the time to bring our country together and begin the orderly
transition of power that has occurred in our nation for more than two

hundred years. The Constitution has triumphed once again."[7] But in the United States, the Constitution is always triumphant because it would be sacrilegious to view it any other way. Republican mobs in Miami, incompetent election officials, self-serving Supreme Court justices—such things merely *look* like symptoms of political breakdown. But if one truly *believes* in an omniscient Constitution, then one knows they are not.

Yet rather than triumphing in November–December 2000, the Constitution merely endured. Rather than proving its omniscience, its performance proved the opposite, i.e. that any device created by fallible beings is itself fallible and hence prone to breakdown and decay.

Unfortunately, the Constitution's performance also proved something else. Despite what it says in the high-school civics texts, the United States is not a democracy. What it is, rather, it is an eighteenth-century republic that has come to resemble a democracy in certain respects, but which at its core remains stubbornly pre-democratic. In stating on December 12 that the individual citizen has no constitutional right to vote for president, the Supreme Court's five-member conservative majority was merely stating what was obvious to anyone who had actually read Article II, which is that the power to choose members of the Electoral College lies with the individual state legislatures rather than the people at large. Yet it couldn't help but come as a shock to the millions of Americans who have come to regard voting in presidential elections as a fundamental democratic right. Now the Supreme Court wished to inform them that such a right did not exist. While the United States might look like a democracy and sometimes even act like one, it was fundamentally a holdover from the days when not even the most radical politicians believed that the people should be free to run the government as a whole.

Civil libertarians who define democracy as a series of "thou shall not's"—thou shall not abridge freedom of speech, thou shall not abridge freedom of the press, and so forth—miss the boat. As important as such liberties may be, modern democracy must be understood first and foremost in terms of the *positive* freedom of the people as a whole to exert effective control over the whole of society. A people's freedom to reshape their entire environment is the freedom on which all others rest. Yet a society in which an unelected judiciary lightly tosses aside the results of a popular election because it would take too much time to tally up the vote is one in which the people's impotence is all too apparent.

THE GORE–BUSH PRESIDENTIAL ELECTION has thus emerged as the great divide. Where Americans were formerly inclined to see the Supreme Court as a neutral body devoted to a concept of the law as a force greater than politics, they now see that it as no less baldly political than any other institution in Washington. Where previously they had looked upon the Electoral College as a harmless relic from another era, they now see that it is not harmless at all, but a serious infringement on the people's right of self-government. But while it is certainly welcome that American eyes have opened at least a crack to the true nature of their ruling institutions, the process would be incomplete if it did not lead to a reexamination of the document from which all these institutions derive, i.e. the US Constitution. The Electoral College is an essential part of a structure assembled more than two centuries ago with utmost rigor and care. The House and Senate, the presidency, the arduous amending process outlined in Article V—these were not items that the Founders lightly tossed onto the table like a deck of playing cards, but elements that they honed and crafted in such a way as to fit together as tightly as pieces in a jigsaw puzzle. If institutions like the Electoral College have resisted reform all these years, it is because Americans sense, not incorrectly, that they are integral to the overall design and that removing them would throw the entire machinery out of whack. As one constitutional scholar put it in the early 1990s, changing the Electoral College might be a good idea, "But it would take a constitutional amendment to change it. And people start to worry that when you tinker with the system, who knows what we'll be left with?"[8] Since tinkering would necessitate rethinking the entire structure, Americans have preferred to leave well enough alone.

But now that the constitutional machinery has been thrown out of whack regardless, Americans may no longer have that option. They increasingly find themselves forced to tackle a problem that previous generations have repeatedly put off. Rethinking the Constitution in the twenty-first century is no easy task. Indeed, it is no less revolutionary than rethinking the solar system was in the sixteenth. Americans do not merely live under the Constitution; they live *in* the Constitution, inhabiting its recesses, shaping their lives according to its needs and dictates, absorbing its logic and making it their own. There is nothing in American society that does not bear the Constitution's stamp in one way or another; if this sounds dogmatic, it is because an entire legal and political system that derives from a single 4,400-word document is itself dogmatic. Rethinking the Constitution as a whole means rethinking the United States as a whole, something Americans have never dared to do.

THIS MEANS LEARNING to view a great deal else differently as well. Take history, an area in which American attitudes are surprisingly complex. Supposedly, Americans are great believers in progress, the idea that people are capable of learning from experience and improving their condition from one year to the next. As much as Americans may admire the ingenuity of a Benjamin Franklin or a Robert Fulton, they know that science and technology have advanced far beyond what those eighteenth-century pioneers could have imagined. But for all their belief in scientific progress, they believe the opposite in terms of constitutional development. Rather than progress and advancement, Americans consider it an article of faith that it is impossible to advance beyond the wisdom of the Founders. As Clinton put it in 1997 in a televised "town hall" meeting in Akron, Ohio:

> We live in a country that is the longest-lasting democracy in human history, founded on the elementary proposition that we are created equal by God. That's what the Constitution says. And we have never lived that way perfectly, but the whole history of America is in large measure the story of our attempt to give more perfect meaning to the thing we started with—the Constitution and the Bill of Rights.[9]

Leaving aside the fact that nowhere does the Constitution state that "we are created equal by God"—the statement is a paraphrase of the Declaration of Independence—this accurately sums up a concept of American history in which "we the people" are constantly circling back to the principles that made them great in the first place. Just as Edmund Burke described a nation as a partnership "between those who are living, those who are dead, and those who are to be born," constitutional development in the United States involves a similar kind of intergenerational partnership between the Framers and those following in their wake.[10] Rather than improving government, Americans see their mission as remaining true to ideas that were present at the creation. Indeed, if Clinton is any authority, the idea is not merely to remain true, but "to give more perfect meaning" to ideas that preceded them by more than two centuries.

But how does one give more perfect meaning to something that was perfect to begin with? Are such efforts superfluous? Or could it be that the Founders' teachings were not perfect after all and that it is the job of subsequent generations to fill in the blanks they left behind? If so, it is a task that Americans feel they must undertake without ever admitting to themselves that is what they are up to. They must deny that the Founders were in any way imperfect and insist that they represented an unsurpassable peak of human wisdom that "we the living" can barely hope to comprehend. Yet they must fix problems that the Founders created. While human knowledge may advance in some areas, any thought of advancing beyond an eighteenth-century level in political science is forbidden.

But if Americans are to come to grips with the Constitution, they must say goodbye to such pre-modern beliefs. They must recognize that progress is not confined to the technological realm, but is something that must take place across the board if it is to take place at all. The lesson of the 2000 presidential election is that the United States is not the most perfect government on earth, but one of the most antique. Its constitutional machinery is woefully obsolete due to generations of neglect. It must be rethought from top to bottom if it is to be hauled into the world of modern democracy.

2

CONCEPTION

ONE OF THE UNFORTUNATE ASPECTS of American-style constitution-worship is that it takes a complex historical process and reduces it to a tale of Moses descending from the mountaintop. Instead of real people trying to work their way through real problems, national mythology has given us a group of tribal patriarchs known as the Founding Fathers participating in what a 1960s best seller described in all seriousness as the "miracle at Philadelphia."[1] The true story of the growth and development of the US Constitution is a good deal richer than any such one-dimensional account would suggest.

The Constitution was the product of two centuries of colonization, revolution, and civil war, a process that began in the late 1500s under Elizabeth I, when England first began gearing up for the invasion of the New World, and concluded two centuries later under George III, when London's clumsy handling of what was by now a rich and far-flung empire caused the biggest piece to break away. As difficult as it is to generalize about such a rich and complex historical epoch, one thing we can safely say is that it was characterized by a wholesale acceleration in the pace of historical development. Great Britain was extending its power from the Caribbean to St. Lawrence, while Westminster was uniting the British archipelago—England, Ireland, Wales, and Scotland—in a common federation headquartered in London. The Bank of England, founded in 1694, was revolutionizing high finance, Sir Isaac Newton was revolutionizing science, writers like Daniel Defoe were revolutionizing literature, while, from the mid-1700s on, cities like Manchester, Birmingham, and Glasgow were revolutionizing production. In 1700, when Britain was still a second-rate power, educated men and women on the Continent had no more reason to learn English than to learn Swedish or Dutch. By the year 1800, the language was fast becoming *de rigueur*.

Another thing we can say about this period is that side by side with this stepped-up pace of development went stepped-up intellectual resistance on the part of those caught up in it. On both sides of the Atlantic, Britons subscribed to a quasi-Newtonian law of conservation in which modernization in one area was seen as being necessarily offset by anti-modernization in another. The more science and economics surged forward, the more important it seemed that other areas, most notably law and politics, remain fixed in place. In legal terms, this period was the heyday of "the Ancient Constitution," the belief that England had been born a freedom-loving nation and would remain one only to the degree that it remained true to its ancient principles. Given that no one had ever written the Ancient Constitution down, the concept was extremely malleable. It could be used to argue for a stronger parliament or for a stronger crown. But it both reflected and reinforced what could be described as democratic primitivism, the belief that ancient times had been freer, that the modern age had witnessed a loss of liberty, and that the way to recapture freedom was to return to the sturdy old principles of the past. The more modernization severed ties with the past in one regard, the more important it seemed to re-establish them in another.

This was not just a theory, moreover, but a mentality, a deeply ingrained habit of thought that colored all perceptions. If freedom was to be attained by returning to ancient principles, then it followed that reform was not a process of moving forward, but a process of purging away all the muck and mire of the modern world so that society could return to its former purity. Rather than new, good government was old, the older the better. As Henry St. John Bolingbroke, leader of a highly influential school of thought known as the "Country" opposition (about which more later), wrote in 1749: "All that can be done ... to prolong the duration of a good government is to draw it back, on every favorable occasion, to the first good principles on which it was founded."[2] Rather than going forward, progress meant the opposite.

In terms of political structure, primitivism of this sort manifested itself in ever more fervent belief in the virtue of checks and balances, separation of powers, and the overriding importance of constitutional balance. Under the Tudors, the dynasty that ruled from 1485 to 1603, England had seen a re-florescence of what political historians call the late medieval constitution. On the Continent, royal absolutism had led to the shutting down of one representative assembly after another. Yet in England, paradoxically, the growth of the monarchy had seen a concomitant growth in the power of a wide range of political institutions. These included not just the two houses of parliament, but other independent power centers such as the Inns of Court, the London law schools that were a stronghold of the common law; the municipal corporations; the church and universities; the City of London, etc. Not only was each such power jealous of its own rights and privileges, which all concerned regarded as existing from time immemorial, but each one believed that national strength depended on respect for the rights of each and every individual part. Only when each element in this complicated political structure was allowed to exercise its time-honored prerogatives could the harmony of the whole be assured. As no less a constitutional theorist than William Shakespeare put it in *Troilus and Cressida*, "when the planets in evil mixture to disorder wander, what plagues, and what portents, what mutiny, what raging of the seas, shaking of earth … rend and deracinate the unity and married calm of states." Unity and calm depended on each body keeping to its own time-honored path and not straying into any other.

Governing such an ornate structure was no easy task. The problem confronting all English monarchs from the sixteenth century on was how to extend their control without exceeding the traditional boundaries of their power. It is a matter of historical controversy, for example, whether Henry VIII, who ruled from 1509 to 1547, was a straightforward absolutist in the Continental manner or a constitutional monarch who, however brutal, went to considerable pains to remain within the law. However much this may sound like an academic fine point, the distinction is an important one since England was alone among the European powers in emerging from the sixteenth century with its representative institutions not only intact, but enhanced.[3] In order to offset the great landed magnates who had plunged the country into the War of the Roses, Henry deliberately set about building up the power of the lesser gentry in the countryside and the merchants and tradesmen in the cities and boroughs. Rather than dissolving parliament, he expanded its membership and piled more and more responsibility on its plate, particularly that of the House of Commons where enthusiasm for Henrician religious "reforms" (i.e. expropriation of the Catholic monasteries) ran high. Elizabeth I, who gained the throne in 1558, was not as politically adept as her father and was more often at odds with parliament than not.[4] But thanks to her victory over the Spanish Armada in 1588, such troubles were forgotten, and she became the very model of an English monarch who, through strength of character and bravery, brings out all that is best in the English people.

But when we enter the seventeenth century, the period in which the English colonization of America begins, the story begins to change. James I, Elizabeth's successor in 1603, was not a Tudor, but a member of a Scottish family known as the Stuarts who inclined to Continental ideas about the divine right of kings to rule with or without their subjects' consent. James still made an effort to defer to local sensibilities, but his son, Charles, who took over in 1625, did not. Beginning in 1629, he dissolved parliament and attempted to rule on his own for more than a decade. Puritan members of parliament and those trained in the common law, categories that largely overlapped, were outraged; it was as if a US president had dismissed the Supreme Court and announced that henceforth he would interpret the Constitution unilaterally. When Charles' foreign policy began to founder and war with Scotland brought the regime to the brink of bankruptcy, the Puritans' deepest convictions were confirmed. Under Elizabeth, England had fought off an invasion by Catholic Spain. But now that Charles had disrupted the age-old balance of power between parliament and the crown, freedom was on the ropes, the patriotic Protestant religion was in retreat, and England's fortunes were waning. The Ancient Constitution had been violated; restoring it in all its glory was the key to setting things to right. By 1641, royalists and Puritan supporters of parliament were actively preparing for war.

HOWEVER ARCANE EVENTS LIKE THESE may seem to modern readers, the extreme antiquity of the US Constitution makes them all too relevant. Although the Jamestown colony, which began in 1607, was strictly a commercial venture, the Massachusetts Bay colony two or three decades later was a direct outgrowth of the deepening constitutional crisis. The Puritan exodus began around the time that Charles was dissolving parliament, and it ceased the moment it became clear that civil war was impending and that Puritan militants were needed in support of the parliamentary cause back home. Many Massachusetts men did indeed return to England to do battle with the crown. Those who did not wound up preserving as if in amber political beliefs characteristic of the period leading up to the great confrontation, but not those that followed.

This is hardly unusual; to one degree or another, emigrants always wind up freezing in place the ideas and images of the society they leave behind. But what was ironic about the New England Puritans is that they did so at a time when the belief system back home was in an especially high state of flux. The English Revolution of the 1640s swung both ways: not only did it topple the crown, but it toppled the beliefs of those who did the toppling. Oliver Cromwell, leader of the parliamentary forces from 1644 on, put Charles on trial for treason against "the fundamental constitutions of this kingdom." But once he had chopped Charles' head off, he proceeded to dissolve both houses of parliament and impose a military dictatorship far more stringent than anything Charles had contemplated. In setting out to restore the ancient balance of power, he ended up creating something close to a modern centralized state. The Ancient Constitution was once more in the ascendant following Cromwell's death in 1658 and the restoration of the crown in 1660, and the old idea of checks and balances, separation of powers, and the like enjoyed particular prestige around the time of the "Glorious Revolution" of 1688–9, when parliament rose in revolt against yet another Stuart absolutist, James II. But the old form of government's victory was only temporary. Even as they were putting the Ancient Constitution back on its pedestal, the English were embarking on a long and fitful process of constitutional modernization that would increasingly concentrate power in the hands of parliamentary leaders acting in behest of the king. The more British leaders extolled the Ancient Constitution and the checks and balances that went with it, the more they wound up violating them.

This was not the case in British North America, however. If "a great deal of what is peculiar in English history is due to the obvious fact that Great Britain is an island," as the historian Sir Lewis Namier once remarked, then a great deal of what is peculiar in US constitutional development is due to the obvious fact that America is a continent.[5] The idea that it was the duty of all good British patriots to remain true to the old forms of government was increasingly unrealistic amid the crowded European power politics of the eighteenth-century when governments had to adapt quickly in order to survive. But it was less unrealistic in the New World. With no enemies in sight except the French in Canada and a scattering of Indians along the western frontier, the colonists had little need for a centralized government, large-scale bureaucracy, or an expensive military establishment. With immense natural resources and a diverse middle-class economy based on farming, shipping, and a scattering of handicraft industries, they had little need for banks, large-scale investment, or other types of high finance. Happily ensconced in an Old English backwater, they could afford to make due with Old English constitutional ideas. The rudimentary forms of government that the Ancient Constitution implied were more than adequate for their needs.

The result was a political structure that was even more pluralistic than the neo-medieval system they had left behind in the early seventeenth century. Rather than a single kingdom, Britain's new western provinces were divided up into thirteen separate "plantations," each with its own governor, bicameral legislature, and *ad hoc* court system. The colonies paid little attention to London thanks to a policy of benign neglect continuing well into the mid-eighteenth century, while, outside of New England, local communities paid little heed to their own colonial governments. Bureaucracy was minuscule, law courts met no more than fifteen to thirty days a year, while legislatures were rarely in session for more than one month out of twelve.[6] The resultant legal structure was a hodgepodge of English common law, parliamentary law, and law made by the local assemblies, the sum total of which, royal governors complained, was enough to leave everyone thoroughly confused as to where their real rights lay.[7] Not only was colonial government fragmented, moreover, but its forms were static and archaic. Where the British parliament was moving boldly into uncharted territory, colonial legislatures still clung to the neo-medieval belief that a legislature's job was not to make new law, but to declare old law by deciding how ancient legal principles were to be interpreted in view of changing circumstances. Thus, the Massachusetts colonial assembly, which still called itself a "court," felt obliged to explain as late as 1761 that three bills it had passed were not new at all, but merely extensions of existing law.[8] New law was suspect, while old law was sturdy and reassuring.

"New England is where old England did stand," declared an anonymous seventeenth-century ditty, "new furnished, new fashioned, new womaned, new manned."[9] New England was better than Old England because it was truer to ancient ways. Although the political culture in Virginia was in many respects the opposite of that of New England, the results there were even more conservative and autarchic. Where Massachusetts at least believed in some form of government, Virginia's royalist gentry believed in being left alone on their own estates to recreate the rural life in England that Cromwell had so rudely interrupted. Virginia was a society frozen in time; even its language was old-fashioned, with words like *bide* (as in "bide awhile"), *howdy, craw* (for "throat"), *tarry, tote, passel, woebegone*, and *grit* (for "courage") lingering on long after they had disappeared from the English countryside.[10] Yet, rather than paying a price for such archaic attitudes, Virginians, like British North Americans generally, wound up prospering. Where Englishmen were allowing a rising Whig aristocracy to rob them of more and more of their ancient liberties, their American cousins were reaping the benefits of remaining true to the Ancient Constitution.

This is what made America such a happy hunting ground for the aforementioned Country opposition. In contrast to a "Court" party composed of financial insiders, high-level Whigs, and parliamentary backbenchers grown fat on royal sinecures and payoffs, the Country party of the late seventeenth century on consisted of all those who felt shut out from the centers of power: backwoods country squires disgusted by the noise and squalor of London, urban tradesmen outraged by the growth of corruption and financial trickery, religious "nonconformists" unable to abide the hypocrisy of the Church of England, and so forth. The Country was in many ways the superior of the two parties. It was more intellectual, more high-minded, perhaps even more moral. But it was also more reactionary. As the historian J.G.A. Pocock has observed of such Country luminaries as Viscount Bolingbroke: "Their language was humanist, their enemy was modernity, and their posture had something of the sixteenth century about it and something of the twentieth."[11] The Country's answer to the growth of corruption, high finance, and political centralization was always the same: bring back the Ancient Constitution, do away with the noxious modern practice of concentrating power in the hands of a "prime minister" and a circle of hand-picked cronies known as a "cabinet," and return to the time-honored separation of legislative, judicial, and executive functions. Parliament should jealously guard its independence. It should serve as a check on the crown and no more. It should concentrate on legislative functions, while insisting that the king concentrate on the executive. Only when the planets returned to their proper orbits would plagues and portents cease rending the unity and married calm of states.

SUCH BELIEFS SHAPED AMERICAN ATTITUDES from the outset. They also set the stage for decades of rising political conflict as British politics began heading off in a direction that seemed to confirm Americans' darkest fears about the nature of political power. Following the death of Queen Anne in 1714, parliament imported a reliably Protestant ruler from the German principality of Hanover to take over the throne. But because the new king, George I, spoke no English and was none too fond of his new realm to begin with, he happily turned over daily governance to the parliamentary leaders who had hired him in the first place. Power increasingly fell into the hands of a Whig leader in the House of Commons named Robert Walpole, who had taken charge of cleaning up the financial mess following the collapse of the South Sea Bubble in 1721. After putting British finances back in order as chancellor of the exchequer, Walpole then proceeded to take over the entire government. Using a secret slush fund among other things, he kept himself in power by cultivating a solid block of parliamentary support for better than two decades. The British intelligentsia regarded him as the very soul of corruption, yet Walpole soldiered on regardless. While the king ruled in name, he and a powerful circle of Whig magnates increasingly ruled in deed.

The upshot was Britain's first parliamentary government, one based not on separation of power, but on a union of legislative, executive, and judicial functions. The Country opposition predicted disaster, yet the efficiency of the new arrangement was apparent for all to see. Across the Channel, ministers fighting desperately to stave off bankruptcy under Louis XVI could only marvel at Britain's ability to borrow money and raise revenue without alienating the moneyed classes or sparking a peasant revolt. Where the old order had made a virtue out of political disunity, the new order marched forward with startling single-mindedness.

This was the world turned upside down. Yet thanks to the lag in political consciousness, the Court's success stimulated the growth of Country ideology all the more. The language of the Country opposition, to quote one historian, was now spoken "not only by bucolic back-benchers from the shires but also by disgruntled placemen and courtiers, the holders of government stock, and the directors of the Bank of England and of the major trading companies"—anyone, that is, who felt put out by the new power structure or put off by the new way of doing business.[12] Opposition, on the other hand, was all the Country was good for; its purely negative ideology rendered it much better at criticizing power than exercising it. Bolingbroke, for example, rejected Walpole's changes *in toto*. No matter how effective they appeared to be, Bolingbroke maintained that altering just one iota of Britain's traditional form of government was dangerously misguided because, "in a constitution like ours, the safety of the whole depends on the balance of its parts." Every last feature of the British constitution had to remain in place so that the structure as a whole could function as it was originally intended. When pressed as to what he would have the government do instead, Bolingbroke could only fall back on ever more grandiloquent celebrations of the Ancient Constitution, "that noble fabric, the pride of Britain, the envy of her neighbors, raised by the labor of so many centuries, repaired at the expense of so many millions, and cemented by such a profusion of blood"—as if effusions like these were any substitute for practical policy.

In truth, the Country was painting itself into a corner. The more it celebrated Britain's Ancient Constitution, the more irrelevant it became in terms of the real issues of the day. But in America, where virtually the entire country felt alienated from the new power centers in London, the political chemistry was different. Because the contradictions of Country ideology were less apparent, the colonists embraced it with stepped-up fervor. It has been pointed out that not everything the Country opposition said was to the Americans' liking. John Trenchard and Thomas Gordon, authors of a sensational series of Country broadsides known as "Cato's Letters," celebrated the virtues of high-density urban development, something that, outside of New England, Americans almost instinctively opposed.[13] Yet Americans nodded in agreement when "Cato" warned that the new centralized forms of government were increasingly dangerous because concentrated power and liberty were forever at odds. Like fire, Trenchard and Gordon wrote, political power "warms, scorches, or destroys according as it is watched, provoked, or increased."[14] The only way to control its inherently tyrannical tendencies was to see to it that it is

> so qualified, and so divided into different channels, and committed to the discretion of so many different men, with different interests and views, that the majority of them could seldom or never find their account in betraying their trust in fundamental instances. Their emulation, envy, fear, or interest [must] always ma[k]e them spies or checks upon one another.[15]

Political power should be fragmented in order to limit the damage it might do—arguments like these fit Americans to a T. They confirmed the colonists' deep belief that if they were free, it was because their almost exaggeratedly pluralistic system of government made them so. If England was unfree, similarly, it had to be because power was increasingly centralized in the hands of a single ruling coterie.

Published in the 1720s, "Cato's Letters" created a sensation from Boston to Charleston. According to the historian Bernard Bailyn, "Independent issues ... were reprinted again and again, referred to and quoted in every possible context in every colony. ... [John Peter] Zenger's *New York Weekly Journal* in the 1730s was a veritable anthology of these extraordinarily popular essays."[16] Bolingbroke was also an American favorite: Thomas Jefferson copied out long extracts from his works into his private notebooks, while John Adams would later agree that he belonged in every gentleman's library.[17] But perhaps most influential was the Baron de Montesquieu, whose *Spirit of the Laws*, written following a visit to London in 1729, painted the British system in classic Country colors as one based on a separation rather than a union of powers. Like many a starry-eyed fellow traveler, Montesquieu, who moved in aristocratic circles in which Bolingbroke's influence was growing, described British government not as it was, but as he wished it to be.[18] Still, Americans, so unfamiliar with the workings of their own government that they had to rely on the word of a visiting Frenchman, regarded his every word as gospel. The more British government deviated from Montesquieu's description of how things supposedly worked in the 1720s, the more they believed it was devolving into tyranny.

The events leading up to 1776 were a clash between constitutional theories that believed that government existed to *conserve* ancient liberties versus those that believed that government had to be free to adapt to the needs of the day. The Seven Years' War of

1756–63, known as the French and Indian War in the US, was the turning point. Where Americans were proud of their contribution to the war, the British authorities were taken aback by the way the colonists had balked at paying taxes and had continued trading with the enemy as if it were some ancient constitutional right. "The Delays we meet with, in carrying on the Service, from *every* part of this country, are immense," Lord Loudon, commander in chief of British forces in North America, wrote to his superiors in London. "In Place of Aid and the Service every impediment, that is possible to invent, is thrown in the Way."[19] The fact that the Americans would especially benefit from the expulsion of the French from Canada made their behavior doubly outrageous in the eyes of the British ruling class. With the conclusion of the war, London resolved to make the Americans toe the line.

THE UPSHOT WAS A POLITICAL HARDENING on both sides. Where Americans had once been favorite sons, they now felt like neglected stepchildren. Beginning in 1763, parliament placed one impediment after another in their way. London prohibited Americans from moving west of the Appalachians so as not to provoke the Indians in the Ohio Valley. It required them to pay a sugar tax whose purpose was to benefit British growers in the West Indies. It ordered the colonies to cede ownership of western lands to the French Canadians, while in 1765 it imposed a stamp tax in direct violation of the old custom of allowing Americans to tax themselves via their local assemblies. The Townshend Acts, passed in 1767, required Americans to pay import duties on lead, glass, paint, paper, and tea so as to benefit British manufacturers. The American colonists constituted roughly twenty-five percent of the British population, yet it now seemed that their interests ran second to French Catholics, Caribbean planters, and the tea merchants of the East India Company. They were a resource for everyone else to exploit.

The nature of politics in London fueled their deepening sense of alienation. Although modern in some respects, British government was still almost flamboyantly antique in others. Because parliament had not seen a general redistricting since Elizabethan times, half-deserted "rotten boroughs" in the south continued to elect members of parliament while new-sprouting metropolises like Manchester in the north did not. This was not supposed to matter since, thanks to the doctrine of "virtual representation," MPs supposedly represented not just their own constituencies, but the empire as a whole. But Americans, clinging to a neo-Elizabethan concept of the legislator as someone whose job was to represent local interests, were unconvinced.[20]

Americans meanwhile found the general atmosphere of corruption and deal making in London to be nothing short of repellent. Where colonists valued honesty, thrift, and self-reliance above all else, the Court used a seemingly endless supply of no-show royal jobs to reward supporters in parliament and secure their loyalty. "Old Corruption," as it was fondly known, was supposedly the grease that kept the wheels of government moving; if so, it greased the wheels for those who could afford to purchase political services while shutting out those who could not. At one point, it was seriously suggested that if Americans really wanted to make themselves heard in London, the best thing would be to emulate wealthy Caribbean planters who had purchased country estates and the legislative seats that went with them and who now constituted a formidable "West India interest" in parliament.[21] But what American would want to move to a place where the richest among them would be nothing more than a poor country relation? Abroad, Benjamin Franklin found his thoughts straying back to "the happiness of New England, where every man is a Freeholder, has a vote in publick Affairs, lives in a tidy warm House, has plenty of good Food and Fewel...."[22] America was not only a different country, but a different way of life. It was home.

THE DECLARATION OF INDEPENDENCE neatly summed up American thinking. In keeping with the humanist aspect of Country ideology, its opening chords were high-minded and rationalist. "[A]ll men are created equal," it proclaimed. "[T]hey are endowed by their Creator with certain unalienable Rights," among which "are Life, Liberty, and the pursuit of Happiness." Given that government derives its authority "from the consent of the governed," it was "the Right of the People to alter or to abolish" government whenever it ceased protecting their rights.

This was in keeping with the very *au courant* notion of popular sovereignty, an idea that existed in embryo in the work of such sixteenth and seventeenth-century theorists as Jean Bodin and Thomas Hobbes, but was only now coming into its own. But then, as it set about explaining why the existing government should be abolished, the declaration shifted gears. Its chief complaint against both George III and parliament was not that they had failed to protect the people's interests, but that they had exceeded their traditional constitutional bounds. The document condemned George III for vetoing the colonial legislatures even though the crown had not vetoed an act of parliament since 1707:

> He has refused his Assent to Laws, the most wholesome and necessary for the public good. ... He has dissolved Representative Houses repeatedly, for opposing with manly firm-ness his invasions on the rights of the people. ... He has

obstructed the Administration of Justice, by refusing his Assent
to Laws for establishing Judiciary Powers.

George, in other words, had subordinated the colonial legislatures to
parliament when the neo-Elizabethan ideology of the Americans
insisted that all such governing institutions should be equal and independent. Violating separation of powers, the declaration went on, had
led to other abuses as well:

> He has made Judges dependent upon his Will alone. ... He has
> kept among us, in times of peace, Standing Armies without the
> Consent of our legislature. ... He has erected a multitude of
> New Offices, and sent hither swarms of Officers to harass our
> People, and eat out their substance.

Echoing Bolingbroke's plea of a quarter-century earlier for a "patriot
king" to preserve constitutional balance by reining in an over-mighty
legislature, the Declaration of Independence, finally, laced into the
monarch for failing to rein in a parliament whose "jurisdiction [is]
foreign to our constitution." Parliament had taxed the Americans
without their consent and curtailed their ability to engage in foreign
trade. It had "tak[en] away our Charters, abolishing our most valuable
Laws, and altering fundamentally the Forms of our Government." Yet
the king had done nothing. Although it was the king's duty to force
parliament to return to its traditional role, he had colluded in forcing
change on unwilling American colonists. By conspiring to rob
Americans of their ancient liberties, George III was guilty of the worst
crime a monarch could commit: tyranny.

The Declaration of Independence accused King George of doing
both too much and too little by vetoing colonial legislatures while
failing to veto parliament back home. Ordinarily, Country ideology

held that the solution to the problem of corruption and tyranny was to force the legislative, executive, and judicial branches to return to their original orbits so that the constitutional balance of power would be restored. But parliament and the crown were beyond Americans' reach. Their only choice was to break away and re-establish proper constitutional balance on their own. To preserve freedom, the colonists would have to recreate the Ancient Constitution out of New World materials.

3

BIRTH

IF THE AMERICAN REVOLUTION were a neat and simple affair of freedom-loving patriots versus an oppressive king, the constitutional arrangements that arose out of it would be a simple affair as well. But it was not. Like the Declaration of Independence itself, the revolution was a mixed bag, forward-looking in some respects, nostalgic and even reactionary in others. In the North, the movement began as a classic bourgeois democratic uprising, an urban-centered upheaval in which townsfolk and their rural allies stood shoulder to shoulder against the crown. South of the Mason–Dixon Line, the rebellion was more complicated. Whereas most whites were patriotic, most blacks were royalist, particularly after Lord John Dunmore, the royal governor of Virginia, issued a proclamation in late 1775 offering freedom to any slave who ran away and joined the loyalist forces. Thousands of black Americans quickly took him up on his offer, including twenty-two belonging to that prophet of equality, Thomas Jefferson.[1] While the North emerged from the revolutionary crucible more democratic than it had been previously, the South emerged more racially polarized, while slavery, as we shall see, emerged strengthened as well. One could argue that, on balance, the revolution was progressive because it gave rise to forces that moved quickly to eliminate slavery in the North and would eventually eliminate it in the nation as a whole. But not only did no one know this at the time, we can safely say that if they had known, planters like Jefferson and James Madison would never have joined the revolution in the first place.

The immediate post-revolutionary period was a mixed bag also. The economy was in ruins thanks to the war and the cut-off in trade with Great Britain, while politics were similarly in disarray. Americans had made for very strange revolutionaries. Rather than uniting against the enemy, they seemed to believe that the best way to keep the flame of freedom burning was to remain as disunited as they could. The states conceded minimal authority to the Continental Congress, which only prevailed in the end because brilliant diplomats like Benjamin Franklin, Arthur Lee, and Silas Deane succeeded in enlisting France and Spain on the American side. Now that independence had been achieved, the states seemed intent on taking back what little of their autonomy they had given up. Little more than a voluntary agreement among sovereign states, the Articles of Confederation, America's first constitution, denied the government the right to impose taxes, regulate trade, raise armies, or suppress insurrections. It left the states free to restrict one another's goods and refuse each other's currency. With New York and New Hampshire engaged in dangerous sword rattling over control of Vermont and Vermont itself contemplating a hook-up with British Canada, it seemed only a matter of time before the entire federation descended into internecine warfare. European powers would pick off the states one by one, and independence would be lost. Impotent from the start, Congress was barely able to muster a quorum to approve the 1783 Treaty of Paris, which ended the war on surprisingly favorable terms to the US, and by 1786 had all but ceased to function.

Some sort of authority was required to prevent the states from flying apart. But authority was politically suspect on the grounds that it tended irretrievably toward tyranny. To understand the predicament Americans found themselves in, consider two efforts at constitution making prior to the Constitutional Convention of 1787. The first occurred in Philadelphia, the biggest city in America and the most polarized. Long at odds with the Quaker establishment, the city's mechanics and tradesmen had seized control of the state government during the first blush of revolution and had used it to push through legislation favorable to people like themselves. Led by individuals like David Rittenhouse, a watchmaker turned scientist; Charles Willson Peale, a poor boy who had risen to become a clockmaker and a silver-smith (and would later become a famous portrait painter); James Cannon, a college teacher and political associate of Tom Paine; and Benjamin Rush, a physician with a practice among the poor, the movement created a constitution in 1776 that was one of the most radical instruments of the entire revolutionary period.[2] It created a unicameral legislature based on near-universal manhood suffrage, guaranteed freedom of speech and the press, and prohibited religious qualifications for office other than a simple belief in God. In contrast to the closed nature of government in London, it promised a government that would be fully open to public view.

This was all quite modern and democratic. But two things about the Pennsylvania Constitution of 1776 stand out. In keeping with Trenchard and Gordon's dictum that power must be "divided into different channels" so as to make the various elements "spies or checks upon one another," the document was careful not only to offset the General Assembly with a separately elected executive council, but to establish a septennial "council of censors" with sweeping powers to investigate every last state official to determine whether "the constitution has been preserved inviolate in every part." It was a recipe for a prosecutorial state in which Kenneth Starr, of Monica Lewinsky fame, would not have felt out of place. In addition, the constitution asserted that "the people of this State have the sole, exclusive and inherent right of governing and regulating the internal policies of the same." Equating popular sovereignty and state autonomy in this manner was a slap in the face of all those who believed that the individual states would have to surrender some of their prerogatives if they were to prevail against the king.

The dynamics in the American Revolution were the opposite in some respects of those of the French Revolution thirteen years later. Where the most democratic elements in Paris were simultaneously the most fervent in preaching national unity, *une et indivisible*, seemingly the most democratic elements in the United States were the most hostile to any suggestion of a unified nation-state, which is why, by the early 1780s, the former colonies were buzzing with petty politicians demanding that the people cast off federal control just as they had cast off British. The second exercise in constitution making occurred in 1781–3 in Virginia when Jefferson, after an unhappy stint as governor, began drawing up plans for a new state government in his spare time. Jefferson's proposed constitution went through three drafts, and although it was never adopted, it is none the less valuable for the insight it offers into the thinking of a certain section of the Virginia squirearchy. Just as Jefferson, with his peculiarly bifurcated intellect, was capable of writing that "all men are created equal" while owning more than a hundred slaves, he was also capable of writing that the people have an unqualified right to abolish government whenever it ceases serving their interests while creating a state government in Virginia based on opposite principles. Unrestrained political power in the hands of the people, he now decided, was the very "definition of despotic government." While he favored a government "founded on free principles," it was simultaneously important that "the powers of government ... be so divided and balanced among several bodies of magistracy, as that no one could transcend their legal limits, without being effectually checked and restrained by the others."[3] The purpose of a constitution was not to promote popular sovereignty, but to restrain popular power so that it flowed toward what Jefferson regarded as freedom and away from "elective despotism."

Rather than a unicameral government like that in Pennsylvania, Jefferson thus favored a classic Country arrangement based on multiple power centers. The longer he worked on his model constitution, the bigger and more elaborate it became. By the time he had finished, it contained no fewer than ten countervailing institutions: a popularly elected lower house, a state senate, an electoral college, a governor, an eight-member council of state to serve as his advisers, a president to oversee the council of state, an independent judiciary, a special "court of impeachments" made up of members of all three branches, a "council of revision" to recommend changes in legislation, and, finally, periodic conventions to change the constitution. This was separation of powers with a vengeance. But if fragmenting power rendered it less dangerous, then why stop at just ten? Why not fifteen or twenty?

Of course, one reason why not is that fragmenting power in such a fashion resulted in government that was nothing short of crippled. Weak government was one reason why Virginia had been unable to mount an effective resistance when a British expeditionary force tore through the state in 1781. Jefferson himself had barely escaped capture, yet the lesson he drew from the experience was not that Americans needed stronger government, but that they needed weaker government to prevent tyranny from rearing its head in the first place. Considering that popular government threatened to be more vigorous than the royal government it replaced, it was even more important that it be checked and balanced to the point of immobility. The people had to be doubly careful to hamstring whatever government they might create.

A GREAT DEAL SEPARATED JEFFERSON and the Philadelphia radicals, but at least two things united them: a shared attachment to checks and balances and a firm belief that freedom required the elevation of state over national interests. There was a third school of thought in America at this time, however, one that stood for the opposite: the primacy of national interests over state. The Federalists are particularly problematic from a modern and especially a Marxist perspective. Because they were mainly upper class, historians across the political spectrum have assumed that they were conservative. Yet the politics of the day were far too complicated to permit any such easy categorization. On the question of whether the people should have direct, untrammeled sway over their local governments, the Federalists were indeed to the right of their opponents. But on the question of the popular role at the national level, they were to the left for the simple reason that local democrats were leery of the very idea of a national government. At a time when democracy was still thought of along Athenian lines as something suited only to a small city-state, the idea of a democracy encompassing the length and breadth of the United States was incomprehensible across the board. The choice, as both Federalists and anti-Federalists saw it, was between local republicanism along either Virginia or Pennsylvania lines or some sort of national federation that would strive for a compromise midway between the two.

As unfashionable as Marxist orthodoxy might be in the early twenty-first century, there is no better example than the infant United States of the centrality of national consolidation to what Marx and

Engels described as the bourgeois democratic revolution. As long as the states remained disunited and autonomous, radical republicanism in Pennsylvania and elsewhere could only grow more parochial. To the degree the people of each state insisted on their "sole, exclusive and inherent right" to manage their own internal affairs, they would lack any political basis on which to involve themselves in the political affairs of others. Not only would slavery in other states remain beyond their purview, but, as a general rule, the more "radical" the politician, the greater his vehemence would be in arguing that each state should concentrate on its own business and leave its neighbors alone.

An American nation-state was thus the essential precondition for the deepening of democracy and the broadening of democratic horizons. Similar dynamics were evident in the field of property rights. Madison's notes on the proceedings at the Constitutional Convention indicate that the Federalists who gathered in Philadelphia in May 1787 were haunted not only by fears of another Cromwellian people's republic rising up in their midst, but by another specter from the seventeenth century as well, that of Leveller-style economic radicalism. The Levellers, of course, were left-wing Protestant radicals during the English Revolution of the 1640s and '50s who not only preached political equality, but at least a degree of economic equality as well. A month into the Philadelphia Convention, Madison delivered a lengthy speech arguing that the hallmark of a well-designed government was its ability to contain the "leveling spirit" (which, interestingly enough, he described as "agrarian" rather than urban) by offsetting it with other forces:

> An increase in population will of necessity increase the proportion of those who labor under all the hardships of life, and secretly sigh for a more equal distribution of its blessings. These

may in time outnumber those who are placed above the feelings of indigence. According to the equal laws of suffrage, the power will slide into the hands of the former. ... How is this danger to be guarded against on republican principles? ... Among other things by the establishment of a body in the government suffi-ciently respectable for its wisdom and virtue....[4]

This embodiment of wisdom and virtue was to be the Senate, designed as an elitist counterweight to popular pressures from below. Political freedom and economic equality were, in Madison's eyes, mutually opposed; the less Americans had of one, the more they would have of the other. This, of course, is the sort of thing that caused progressive historians like Charles Beard to grind their teeth. But once again, the question of the Federalists as economic royalists is not so simple. In what was still largely a smallholders' republic, property rights were universally popular; if Federalists defended them to the hilt, so did their radical opponents. Moreover, property rights were far from reac-tionary at a time when feudal restrictions on the individual's ability to dispose of his own land, goods, and labor were the chief impediments to economic development.

The property question was also politically volatile in a way that few, if any, Americans at the time recognized. Safeguarding private property in the form of land and goods was one thing. But what about private property in the form of slaves—should that be safeguarded, too? What about the rights of labor? Could workers collectively with-hold their labor so as to force wages up? Or did employers' property rights allow them to band together to force them down? As long as America remained nothing more than a string of scattered, under-developed statelets, such issues would remain dormant. But the more the states were forced to participate in a dynamic national economy, the more they would rise to the fore. The Federalists, stolid men of property though they were, were helping to accelerate development and speed up capitalist contradictions by creating a unified republic, whereas, by opposing such a republic, their allegedly more radical opponents were attempting to slow them down.

APART FROM THEIR NATIONALIST BELIEFS, the Federalists were an otherwise diverse set of merchants, lawyers, and slaveowners facing a particularly diverse and knotty set of problems. Chief among them was how to create anything resembling a unified nation-state out of a disparate group of former British colonies. Mini-states like Delaware and New Jersey felt hemmed in by giants like New York and Pennsylvania, while planters in Virginia and the Carolinas who produced agricultural staples geared for export feared becoming captives of New England shippers and merchants. The political differences were similarly daunting. The Puritans of Massachusetts and the Quakers of Pennsylvania were the descendants of Roundheads who had put Charles I to death in 1649, while the Virginia planters were descendants of royalists who had remained so devoted to the crown that a grateful Charles II had dubbed Virginia his "Old Dominion" on resuming the throne in 1660. As much as a wealthy New Yorker like Gouverneur Morris might seem to have in common with a wealthy South Carolina planter like Pierce Butler, there was a great deal that drove them apart. Unrepentant elitist that he was, Morris informed his fellow delegates that they should put all thoughts of political equality aside in forging a new constitution because "there never was, nor ever will be a civilized society without an aristocracy." But when Butler told the convention a short time later that the labor of any one of his slaves "was as productive and valuable as that of a freeman in Massachusetts," Morris bristled. If slaves were as productive as freemen, then why had Northerners bothered to cast their chains off in 1776?[5] Why had the revolution even been fought? Class lines in America cut vertically and horizontally, dividing not only rich and poor, but incipient bourgeois elements up North from neo-feudalist planters down South. Yet if the Constitutional Convention was to be successful, delegates would have to put aside such differences for the duration. They would have to find a way, however temporary, of bridging the unbridgeable.

Another problem the convention confronted was that of mandate. Each delegation had been selected by its own state legislature. But did that mean they were empowered to speak in behalf of their states alone or for the nation as a whole? Although the Continental Congress had authorized a convention "for the sole and express purpose of revising the Articles of Confederation," the delegates quickly cast the Articles aside and began work on a different document entirely. But where did the authority for such a rash act come from if not from the Continental Congress? One answer might have been from the people at large, but, as several delegates pointed out, the people were largely absent from the constitution-making process. "Much has been said about the sentiments of the people," Gouverneur Morris observed "They were unknown. They could not be known. All that we can infer is that if the plan we recommend be reasonable and right; all who have reasonable minds and sound intentions will embrace it."[6] Yet according to another delegate, Elbridge Gerry of Massachusetts, reasonable minds at that point were exceedingly scarce. The people of his state, he informed the convention, "have at this time the wildest ideas of government in the world. They were fore abolishing the senate in Massachusetts and giving all the other powers of government to the other branch of the legislature."[7] Rather than representing the people, the delegates were legislating in behalf of a hypothetical "reasonable man" whom they hoped that a new constitution would call into existence.

This is another way in which American political dynamics differed from those of the French. The Philadelphia convention did not take place in an open hall, the galleries packed with sansculottes hooting or applauding as they saw fit. To the contrary, the delegates deliberated behind closed doors while the people went about their business outside. Arguably, this bespeaks the difference between volatile Frenchmen and businesslike Americans less interested in grandstanding than in getting the job done. But it also bespeaks the difference between evolving French and Anglo-American concepts of democracy. In France after 1789, the masses were omnipresent. No matter who was on top at any given moment, everyone was constantly aware of their immense power. In America, by contrast, popular power was more theoretical. While the Philadelphia delegates believed they knew what the people wanted (or at least what the people would accept), they could never be quite sure because the popular voice was scattered and muffled. Instead of creating a new political order on their own, the unstated assumption throughout was that the people would confine themselves to approving or disapproving schemes that others drew up in their behalf. While perhaps apocryphal, the oft-told tale of an old woman confronting Benjamin Franklin as the Constitutional Convention was drawing to a close is nonetheless telling. "Well, doctor," the woman supposedly demanded, "what have you given us?" "Madam," Franklin replied, "we have given you a republic, if you can keep it." A constitution was not something that the people created themselves, but something that a few outstanding individuals created for them. Now that Moses had brought the law down from the mountaintop, it was up to the Israelites to demonstrate that they were worthy of receiving it.

Popular power in the new republic expressed itself in largely negative terms. Aware that Americans had already risen in revolt against attempts at "altering fundamentally the forms" of their archaic democracy, the delegates were anxious not to provoke them again. "The people have been long accustomed to this right [to vote] in various parts of America, and will never allow it to be abridged," Nathaniel Gorham of Massachusetts warned the delegates in August. "We must consult their rooted prejudices if we expect their concurrence in our propositions."[8] Elbridge Gerry cited a similar reason in opposing a proposal to establish a standing army, an old Country bugaboo. "The people," he said, "would not bear it." So how were the delegates to impose change on such a change-averse polity? The answer was to make it seem that whatever changes they came up with were nothing more than an attempt to re-establish the constitutional equilibrium that the combined power of parliament and the crown had tried so hard to disrupt. The purpose of government was to reinstate natural laws that should never have been violated in the first place. Thus, John Dickinson of Delaware, according to Madison's notes, "compared the national system to the solar system, in which the states were the planets, and ought to be left freely in their own proper orbits," while Madison himself argued a day later that unless something was done to "control the centrifugal tendencies of the states," they would "fly out of their proper orbit and destroy the order and harmony of the political system." The purpose of the new republic was to return the constituent elements to their proper paths so that freedom could once again thrive.[9] The hallmark of a well-made constitution was the degree to which it harmonized with natural law. Rather than making new law, the delegates' job was to discover and reinstate law that was pre-existing.

In a sense, the new political science of which people like Madison and Dickinson were so proud had arisen in response to a single problem: how to bring order out of chaos. If "the turbulence and follies of democracy" were running at high tide throughout the states, as another Federalist, Edmund Randolph of Virginia, told the Philadelphia convention, the problem before the delegates was how to tame the beast or at least channel its passions so that they would do no harm.[10] In Britain, the classic solution, espoused by Court and Country alike, had been to make use of the natural tension among the three great estates, the monarchy, nobility, and Commons, to create a national structure more stable than any one of the three estates standing alone. Yet the Philadelphia delegates faced a special difficulty in this regard: in the absence of a king, an aristocracy, or even an established church, they had to figure out a way of creating a stable structure out of one estate alone: the people.

One solution might have been to jettison the idea of separate estates altogether and concentrate political power in a single national assembly representing the people as a whole. But, as we have seen, balancing an entire national edifice on a single base of support in this manner struck the delegates as madness, a recipe for anarchy, dictatorship, or both. Instead, they groped their way toward a solution in which the people's power would be divided up in imitation of the old estates and then recombined in such a way that was stronger than the original. Rather than decrying divisions within the body of the people, the idea was to make use of such divisions to bind the whole together more fully. New Jersey's demand for equal representation in the legislative branch, consequently, was less troublesome than it might have initially seemed. In essence, it was insisting on a special role for the states *qua* states. But where Hamilton complained that equal state representation regardless of population "shocks too much the ideas of justice and every human feeling," others sensed that the idea was not without its advantages.[11] An enhanced state role would provide them with an additional building block to work with. The more such building blocks they had, the more ways they had of separating and then re-joining popular power so as to create a durable national edifice.

The problem of state versus national citizenship provided them with a similar opportunity. As federal citizens, the delegates agreed that Americans should have the right to elect directly at least one governing institution, which is to say the House of Representatives. Simultaneously, however, they decided that it would only be as citizens of the states that the people would be empowered to define precisely who the people might be. Thus, the delegates agreed that voters in congressional races "shall have the Qualifications requisite for Electors of the most numerous Branch of the State Legislature," i.e. the lower house (Article I, section 2). When it came to the Senate, the delegates agreed that the people should have no right as federal citizens to elect members at all. Instead, they decided that the people should limit their own power to choosing state legislators who would then elect members of the Senate. Since a popularly elected "chief magistrate" might all too easily turn into a populist demagogue, the delegates opted for an even more complicated scheme in regard to the executive branch. The people of each state, they decided, would vote for state legislators who would then vote for members of the Electoral College, who would then vote for president. Instead of one step removed, the people would be two. Of course, the people would be even further removed from a federal judiciary chosen by an indirectly elected president with the advice and consent of an indirectly elected Senate. Considering that judges would "hold their Offices during good Behavior" (Article III, section 1), which effectively meant for life, this was perhaps worrisome. But Hamilton assured Americans that the judiciary would constitute the federal government's "least dangerous branch" since its role would be limited to interpreting a constitution that the people could then amend—again, indirectly—with the approval of two-thirds of each house of Congress plus simple majorities in three-fourths of the state legislatures.[12]

Indirect methods were better because, by turning popular power against itself, they allowed the Federalists to create a national structure that would rise higher and higher. Still, where Jefferson had come up with ten separate power centers in 1783, the Philadelphia Convention, a bit more sensitive to the need for vigorous government, was able to cut that number down to just six: a House and Senate, a presidency, a judiciary, an Electoral College, and a Constitutional Convention that, even if never called, would forever loom as a possibility. The federal government had not won the right to unilaterally countermand state laws, as Madison and Hamilton, the convention's two prime movers, had wished. But the proposed new plan of government gave federal judges the power to strike down state laws on constitutional grounds, while Article VI required all state and federal officials to take an oath of allegiance to the new Constitution as "the supreme law of the land." If the states were not necessarily subservient to the federal government, both were subservient to a common body of constitutional law. In contrast to the profoundly impotent Continental Congress, the proposed new Constitution empowered Congress to regulate foreign and domestic commerce, impose tariffs, levy taxes, establish a national currency, award patents and copyrights, suppress insurrections, and create a standing army and navy. These were powers that either had not existed or the states had hoarded for themselves. Even more remarkably, Article I, section 10, contained a long list of things that the states would henceforth be forbidden to do, such as entering into alliances with one another without congressional consent, overriding or limiting freedom of contract, interfering with domestic or foreign trade, or maintaining their own separate armed forces. These had been some of the chief weapons in the state arsenal, but now they would be taken away.

Assuming that the new constitution would be ratified, this was a dramatic achievement. But such gains came at a price. While limiting divisive forces at one level, the Constitution entrenched them at another. As Madison confided in a letter to his mentor Jefferson a few days after the close of the Constitutional Convention: "*Divide et impera*, the reprobate axiom of tyranny, is under certain conditions, the only policy, by which a republic can be administered on just principles."[13] Power had to be divided so that the worst impulses of the 1780s could be conquered. But what Madison failed to consider is that while tyrants might divide and conquer a subject population, the Constitution was calling upon a supposedly sovereign people to divide and conquer themselves. But this begged the question of how self-imposed disintegration could lead to re-integration. Wouldn't fragmentation lead to still more fragmentation?

We can appreciate this problem more fully if we consider it from the point of view of political sovereignty. The concept of sovereignty had changed dramatically since the sixteenth century. Previously, politicians and theorists had thought of it as more or less synonymous with political power. If the King of France was sovereign on one level, then the Duke of Anjou was sovereign on another, while some other local potentate might be sovereign on a third. The political structure was conceived of as a kind of ladder of ascending sovereignties with God at the top, the king one step below, the lord one step below him, and so on. While it sounds simple, however, the reality was exceedingly complex. When one sovereign lord came into conflict with another, as they invariably did, conflict over whose power was to reign supreme was the inevitable consequence, which is one reason why the feudal system was one of growing warfare.

But then, in the sixteenth century, Jean Bodin, a French political theorist searching for a solution to the kingdom's endemic civil wars, came up with a startling innovation. Sovereignty was not just power, he argued, but *supreme* power. Rather than a big sovereign among many little ones, the king had to be understood as the sole earthly sovereign, at least as far as his own realm was concerned, not just a source of authority, but the sole source from which all authority flowed. Rather than exercising authority in their own right, local lords exercised power in behalf of the king. Conflicts among various contending powers would be impossible in such a system because no one other than the monarch would exercise independent power. Bodin's theory, published in 1576 in a treatise he entitled *Six Livres de la République*, was then picked up and updated in the 1640s and '50s by an Englishman named Thomas Hobbes, a thinker of such unsettling views that he succeeded in alienating both sides in the English Civil War. In contrast to nearly all Anglo-Saxon political thinking to date, Hobbes argued in his masterpiece *Leviathan* (1651) that compacts between separate and sovereign powers such as parliament and the crown were useless as means of achieving political stability. In the absence of an active higher authority capable of imposing order, such agreements would inevitably break down under the pressure of changing circumstances, allowing the old rivalries to reassert themselves. The only way for individuals "to defend them[selves] from the invasion of foreigners, and the injuries of one another," Hobbes wrote, was "to confer all their power and strength upon one man, or upon one assembly of men that may reduce all their wills, by plurality of voices, unto one will."[14] Instead of placing their faith in paper agreements, they had to surrender to nothing less than a "mortal god," some individual or body that would not be subordinate to law, but would be exempt from the law in order to make law for others to obey.[15] Checks and balances would be superfluous in such an arrangement. Instead of separation of powers, the sovereign would combine executive, legislative, and judicial functions in one. Drastic as the consequences might sound, Hobbes maintained that such concentration was the only way to break a vicious cycle of deadlock and breakdown culminating in *bellum omnium contra omnes*, the famous war of all against all.

Hobbes was a dangerous freethinker who would always be at odds with respectable opinion. His concept of sovereignty was antithetical to the notion of an Ancient Constitution and a common law as something that men must subordinate themselves to so that freedom could flourish. None the less, his teachings had enormous impact. In the early seventeenth century, Sir Edward Coke, the leading jurist of the day, had declared that no man ought to think himself wiser than the law because the law represented the accumulated wisdom of the ages that was greater than the power of any one individual.[16] But although they looked upon Coke as something of a hero, members of Cromwell's Long Parliament in the 1640s broke with this notion by underscoring the right of each new parliament to decide for itself irrespective of what others had decided in the past. Rather than subordinating themselves to the past, men were free to head off in entirely new directions. The upshot was a new concept of the "crown-in-parliament" that argued that once the king, the House of Commons, and the House of Lords agreed on something, there was no force, including that of legal precedent, capable of holding them back. While most people still clung to some concept of an Ancient Constitution, the Ancient Constitution was now seen establishing the crown-in-parliament as the "supreme, irresistible, absolute, uncontrolled authority" that the eminently conservative jurist Sir William Blackstone defined in the 1760s as the essence of sovereignty. Because the ancient law said parliament was sovereign, it *was* sovereign, although whether parliament was sovereign vis-à-vis the ancient law was a question that few commentators choose to ask.

Elsewhere, Hobbes' concept met with a mixed reception. In France, not only did the revolutionaries who took power in 1789 not quarrel with sovereignty *per se*, but in taking it away from the crown and placing it in the hands of the people, they emancipated it all the more. Suddenly, the new people's government was able to accomplish things—abolish the old provinces, institute a new system of measurement, impose a *levée en masse*—that would have staggered the imagination of even Louis XIV. Yet in British North America, settled before the Anglo-Saxon concept of parliamentary sovereignty had taken hold, the American revolutionaries did the opposite. After fighting against the combined power of parliament and the king, they were determined to prevent any such force from asserting itself in the New World ever again. As a result, the polity that the delegates to the Constitutional Convention set about constructing in 1787 was a determinedly anti-Hobbesian one in which no single element would reign supreme. Instead, the Federalists engineered their system in such a way that the various elements would continually reduce one another to a common level. While the president could veto an act of Congress, Congress could override him with a two-thirds majority in both houses. While the Supreme Court could strike down presidential or congressional acts it deemed unconstitutional, the other two branches could punish the Supreme Court by impeaching its members or appointing new ones. Where the federal government would be superior to the states by virtue of its ability to impose taxes and regulate trade, the states would be superior to the federal government by virtue of their power to elect senators, representatives, and president. In truth, each constituent element would be simultaneously superior and inferior to every other.

Was this clever or merely confused? As a young Henry Adams would write during the opening months of the Civil War:

> Supreme, irresistible authority must exist somewhere in every government—[this] was the European belief. … America, on the other hand, asserted that the principle was not true; that no such supreme power need exist in a government; that in the American government none such should be allowed to exist, because absolute power in any form was inconsistent with freedom, and that the new government should start from the idea that the public liberties depended upon denying uncontrollable authority in the political system in its part or its whole.[17]

But if the new republic was determined to banish sovereignty, then who, ultimately, would be in charge? The answer was everyone and no one. *The essence of the American system was its fundamental ambiguity as to where ultimate authority lay.* The federal government, the states, and the individual could all lay claim to sovereignty in a way that was plausible, but never entirely conclusive either. They could plausibly deny others' claims to sovereignty in the same way. Initially, it seemed as if the Americans might be on to something in rejecting sovereignty in this fashion as something indivisible and absolute. By returning to a neo-medieval concept of limited sovereignty in the context of a people's republic, they were inviting, in effect, every last citizen (every white, male citizen, that is) to become his own limited sovereign in his own limited domain by becoming a boss, land baron, plantation owner, etc. It was an invitation that every last person, it seemed, strove to fulfill. The results could be fractious, to be sure, but at the same time were almost manically energetic.

On another level, however, the results were paralyzing. When the system as a whole was in crisis, people could only stand by helpless because no one was in charge overall. Where the *herrenvolk* democracy of the Jacksonian era led to an explosion of economic activity, it also gave rise to the Nullification Crisis of 1832–3, the start of a process of political collapse that would culminate in the Civil War. The result was a fundamentally religious society in which the people, due to their own political incapacity, trusted to some higher force to hold together their system of limited sovereignty on their behalf. The more unstable it became, the more fervently they prayed.

DESPITE THE PRAISE heaped upon it over the centuries, the plan of government that emerged out of the Philadelphia Convention was riddled with contradictions and inconsistencies. Consider, for example, the question of the relationship between the people and the plan of government they had allegedly created. The Preamble declares:

> We the People of the United States, in Order to form a more perfect Union, establish Justice, insure domestic Tranquility, provide for the common defence, promote the general Welfare, and secure the Blessings of Liberty to ourselves and our Posterity, do ordain and establish this Constitution for the United States of America.

At first glance, this would seem to advance a clear and unequivocal concept of popular sovereignty, one recognizing "we the people" as having both the power and the right to "ordain and establish" new constitutions whenever they are required to promote welfare and secure liberty. Indeed, considering that the people were preparing to ratify the new constitution in a way that directly violated the precepts of the old—where the Articles of Confederation stipulated that all thirteen states must approve any constitutional change, Article VII of the new Constitution declared that it would consider itself ratified when approved by just nine—the Preamble implicitly recognized the people's ability to overthrow existing constitutions in the process. The people were the all-powerful creator and destroyer. While they could voluntarily submit to laws of their own devising, no one else could force them to do so against their will. The only ones who could force them were the people themselves.

So the Preamble seemed to suggest. A few paragraphs later, though, the Constitution did exactly what the Preamble says a constitution cannot do by requiring the people to submit to laws beyond their power to change. Article I, for example, forbade the people's representatives to interfere with the slave trade for a fully twenty years after ratification. It forbade them to suspend *habeas corpus* other than in times of rebellion or invasion or to pass bills of attainder designed to punish individuals without benefit of trial. Article IV, section 3, forbade the people's representatives from breaking up or merging the individual states without each state's approval, while Article V forbade the people to alter so much as a comma in the new Constitution without first submitting to a tortuous amending process. Two-thirds approval by each house of Congress plus majority approval in three-fourths of the states was better than the unanimous approval required by the Articles of Confederation. But it still placed obstacles in the people's way where the Preamble implied there should be none.

Moreover, Article V ended on an especially problematic note by stipulating that "no State, without its Consent, shall be deprived of its equal Suffrage in the Senate." More than a mere obstacle to the exercise of popular power, this was an insuperable barrier. What it meant, in effect, was that any modification of the sacred rule of equal state representation was forbidden unless every last state gave its consent. Where the two-thirds/three-fourths rule meant that four states representing as little as ten percent of the US population as of 1790 could veto most constitutional amendments, this final clause allowed just one state, representing as little as 1.6 percent of the population, to veto any effort to reform the Senate in accord with the principle of one person-one vote. Given the sheer impossibility of gaining unanimous state approval for any such project, the result to permanently limit the people's power in regard to at least one of their governing institutions.

How was it possible for the Constitution to declare that the people's power was limited on one hand and unlimited on another? The answer is that it wasn't possible, yet the mystique of the Constitution rested on the illusion that it was. For social peace to be maintained, it was essential that the people recognize the Constitution as "the supreme law of the land" vis-à-vis even the popular will. The people had to subordinate themselves to something they had themselves created. It was precisely the sheer impossibility of such an enterprise that imbued the Constitution with a certain religious quality virtually from the outset. For the Constitution to be successful, "we the people" had to believe that it made the impossible real.

BUT THE PUZZLES AND AMBIGUITIES do not stop there. The Constitution could be said to be at war with itself only if the Preambles truly established the people, *une et indivisible*, as the sovereign power. But did it really? Certainly, the words "We the People of the United States … do ordain and establish this Constitution for the United States of America" suggested as much since they seemed to establish the people as the driving force behind the Constitution as a whole. But on closer examination, it was no longer so clear. Take the opening phrase, "We the People of the United States." From a modern perspective, its meaning seems unmistakable: the people of a single nation-state known as the USA. But prior to the Civil War, "United States" was not used as a single noun, but as a plural: the United States *are* rather than the United States *is*. Rather than a single entity, the first requirement of a sovereign power, this suggests that Constitution regarded "we the people" as a collection of separate entities, "we the people of the separate states," sovereign individually, perhaps, but not collectively.

Then there are all those phrases that follow—"in order to form a more perfect Union, establish Justice, insure domestic Tranquility," and so forth. What did these words *mean*? Were they nothing more than a rhetorical flourish meant to convey the unbounded nature of the people's power? Or were they meant to suggest that the people could exercise their awesome power only for certain limited goals? If so, this would imply that the people are not sovereign because sovereignty by definition is unlimited. Of course, one could argue that formulas like "promote the general Welfare" and "secure the Blessings of Liberty" are so vague and general as not to amount to limits at all. But what about the curious words "to form a more perfect Union," which, after "we the people," are probably the most oft-quoted phrase in the entire document? Grammatically, the phrase is meaningless. "Perfect," after all, is an absolute, not a relative quality. But considering the state of American society at the time it was written, it was also strangely unrealistic. Government had ceased to exist, the army was in mutiny, and at least one serious revolt had broken out the previous year in New England. The United States had reached "almost the last stage of national humiliation," as Hamilton would later put it.[18] Yet as a condition of exercising their power, the Preamble seemed to demand that the people agree that the country had already attained one level of perfection and would soon attain one even higher once the new Constitution had taken effect.

Rhetorical analysis of this sort is not mere nitpicking. The question of whether "we the people" were collectively or individually sovereign as citizens of the separate states was the root cause of the Civil War, which led to some 600,000 deaths and destroyed much of the American South. Odd phrases like "to form a more perfect Union" are similarly important for anyone seeking to uncover a constitutional grammar governing how Americans feel and think. If popular sovereignty was never more than a fiction, then it appears that the Preamble was creating a half-formed national persona out of bits and pieces and imbuing it certain qualities. It was programming it, so to speak, to think of the republic in a certain way, which is as something that would unfold ever more brilliantly over time—if, that is, the people remained true to the Constitution that had called them into being. It required them to suspend disbelief and subscribe to the paradox of ever-greater American perfection. For anyone seeking the source of America's famous optimism or the distinctively American belief that America is always moral and just even when it is behaving abominally, then this could be an important linguistic clue.

Of course, a mere slip of paper cannot call an entire people into being. In reality, the American people were calling themselves into being, but in a partial and incomplete form. They were programming themselves to think and believe one way and not another. The very essence of the political project known as "the United States of

America" required that they freeze themselves in a self-contradictory state of semi-sovereignty and not go all the way.

OF THE FIFTY-FIVE DELEGATES who gathered in Philadelphia in 1787, only one, Alexander Hamilton, had any sense of what was at stake. Born a "bastard brat of a Scotch pedlar" (to quote John Adams) in the Danish Virgin Islands in 1757, Hamilton was an *arriviste* even by American standards. But once he came to New York in his mid-teens and threw himself into the revolutionary crisis that was just then unfolding, his abilities were immediately apparent. Not only was he ambitious, intelligent, and a skilled administrator, but as the only one of the half-dozen most important Founders who was not native born, he had an outsider's ability to size up the American situation in its entirety and to think globally and strategically. In essence, he believed that an independent American republic had an opportunity to establish itself as the dominant power in North America and hence as a major player in world politics. To do so, however, it would have to place itself on a proper footing. All but impervious to Country cant about limited government, separation of powers, and the like, Hamilton believe that the first task was to create a sovereign government capable of taking charge of society as a whole and reconstructing it along more competitive lines. Rather than something concerned with establishing just the right balance and harmony among the various constituent elements, he conceived of government in far more modern terms as a machine that would transform those elements and propel society forward.

Although Hamilton played a major role in the events both preceding and following the Philadelphia Convention, his role in the convention itself was minimal. One reason had to do with the way the convention was organized. Because each state delegation voted as a unit, the other New Yorkers, who were all anti-Federalist, voted him down repeatedly and saw to it that his influence was nil. But even if they hadn't voted him down, his views were so at odds with those of the delegates as a whole as to render him all but irrelevant. Just how much at odds became evident in mid-June when the delegates cleared some time for him to present his ideas concerning the shape a new American government should take. Hamilton began with a few simple propositions. The states, he declared, were guilty of elevating their own petty interests above those of the nation. They were filled with demagogues who "hate the control of the general government" and were determined to beat it back at all costs. Yet Congress had shown itself powerless to respond. How, he asked, were such evils to be combated? "Only by [creating] such a complete sovereignty in the general government as will turn all the principles and passions above mentioned on its side." Quickly sketching out his proposal, Hamilton called for a national assembly elected every three years by the people at large, a lifetime elected senate, and a supreme national governor, also elected for life, with a complete and unqualified veto over both the national legislature and the states.[19]

It was ideas like these that earned Hamilton a reputation for Bonapartism at a time when Napoleon was still an unknown officer in the artillery. None the less, his ideas were actually less authoritarian than what the convention as a whole would eventually come up with. Although members of his proposed senate would be elected for life, they would be elected in equal-sized districts rather than state by state. The principle of one person-one vote, the *sine qua non* of modern democracy, would thus have applied in both legislative houses instead of just one. His plan would not have counted slaves as three-fifths of a person for purposes of congressional representation, which by 1860 would give slaveowners some twenty-five extra votes in the

House and the Electoral College. Because Hamilton's proposed government would have been sovereign over the nation, moreover, it would have been sovereign over the constitution, which means that there would have been no question of tiny national minorities holding up constitutional reform generation after generation. The government would be supreme over the constitution rather than vice versa.

To be sure, a lifetime president armed with unlimited veto powers is a shock to democratic sensibilities. But so is (or should be) a constitution that is effectively beyond the people's ability to alter or reform. Hamilton's proposal would have made short work of states' rights by placing responsibility for the nation as a whole, including responsibility for the conduct of national elections, firmly in federal hands. It would have given rise to a system of national politics that would be more dynamic and hence more democratic. Since there would no longer be any argument as to whether sovereignty should or should not exist—Hamilton's constitution would have cleared away any confusion at the outset—the only argument would be over who was to exercise it. A Hamiltonian government would have set the stage for a struggle for power, a prolonged test of wills, between the national assembly and the chief executive. Assuming that the latter post had gone to Washington, the American Joshua who had led his people into the Promised Land, the advantage would have initially been his. But the longer Washington remained in office, the staler his mandate would grow, while that of the assembly would be triennially replenished. Increasingly the focus of democratic hopes and passions, the assembly's standing in the people's eyes would rise as the executive's fell. However speculative it may be, we can imagine the executive withering away to mere figurehead status while real power increasingly passed into the hands of the popular assembly. The ultimate result would be something that America still does not enjoy more than two centuries later: a democratic, sovereign government with untrammeled sway over the nation as a whole.

A different political structure would have led to a different class structure. The anti-Hobbesian system that emerged out of the Philadelphia Convention gave rise to a class system by the 1820s and '30s that was at once radical and conservative. America was more democratic than Northern European nations. Outside of the Deep South where steep property requirements were in effect, it gave nearly all white men the vote. Yet rather than demanding sovereignty over the whole of society, American workers were content to demand equality under the Ancient Constitution. Rather than subordinating the Constitution to their needs, they subordinated their needs to those of the Constitution. The consequence was a budding labor movement that was reverential toward the Founding Fathers (minus the arch-villain Hamilton of course), jingoistic (since the Constitution was the greatest such document in the world, the United States had to be the greatest country), and firmly tied to the Democratic Party at the time when it was a vehicle for Southern slaveholders.

Sovereign national government, on the other hand, would have made for a very different dynamic. In seeking political power, America's swelling ranks of urban laborers would not have been seeking an equal place for itself under the constitutional umbrella, but would have necessarily launched itself on a quest for sovereignty over society and everything in it, including the Constitution. Instead of returning society to the Founders' original vision, its goals would have been transformative—to move American society, in other words, toward something new. Such a movement would have been less "American," which is to say less inclined to see itself as part of a breed apart, and hence more inclined to see its interests as linked to those of workers in other nations. It would have been less inclined to debilitating notions of American exceptionalism and less likely to reject foreign ideologies merely because they were foreign. By leaving it to the states to control federal elections, the Constitution of 1787 provided plebeian whites with a powerful incentive to disenfranchise free blacks, who routinely voted Federalist, so that they could more effectively monopolize state politics. But by eliminating any special role for the states, a powerful national assembly chosen according to uniform voting rules throughout the republic would have done away with any such local monopolies. It would have provided lower-class whites in the North with an incentive to reach out to blacks in the South so as to form a common alliance against the grandees on both sides of the Mason–Dixon Line. As Norman Thomas observed in 1963: "Had we in the United States had a centralized parliamentary government rather than a federal presidential government, we should have had, under some name or other, a moderately strong socialist party."[20] By the same token, a constitutionally entrenched system of limited government all but guaranteed that the United States would remain a society in which socialism would make limited headway.

ONCE THEY HEARD HAMILTON OUT, the delegates, so far as we can tell from Madison's notes, never referred to his plan again. Instead, they returned to the business of creating a kind of political solar system in which the various governing institutions would remain in their own proper orbits *ad infinitum*. Yet Hamilton not only embraced the final document wholeheartedly, but played a leading role in winning ratification.

Why? The answer can be summed up in three words: necessary and proper. In the list of powers that the proposed Constitution gave to the new Congress, the Founders had tacked on a curious provision, one that also empowered it "[t]o make all Laws which shall be necessary and proper for carrying into Execution the foregoing Powers, and all other Powers vested by this Constitution in the Government of the United States, or in any Department or Officer thereof." An expansive reading of this clause suggested that not only was Congress empowered to impose taxes and regulate commerce, but it was empowered to implement the sweeping goals set forth in the Preamble as well. Since such powers had not only been vested in the government of the United States but were its very *raison d'être*, Congress had *carte blanche* to do what it wanted to establish justice, insure domestic tranquility, and promote the general welfare. Given that there was virtually nothing that could not be justified under such a rubric, Hamilton believed that the phrase provided a basis for what he had long been seeking, a federal government of unrestrained power and reach.

Subsequent events proved him wrong. Nearly from the moment Hamilton took over as Washington's *de facto* prime minister in 1789, he found his way increasingly blocked by outraged Southern agrarians who believed, not incorrectly, that his policies represented a threat to their way of life. Increasingly alarmed by Hamilton's ambitious economic plans, Madison, by now a congressman from Virginia, took to the floor of the House in early 1791 to denounce Hamilton's proposal for a national bank not on the grounds it was bad policy, but that it was unconstitutional. A war of memos erupted in Washington's cabinet over the precise meaning of "necessary and proper." Where Hamilton argued that the clause allowed the federal government to do whatever it wanted to in pursuit of the broad goals set forth in the Preamble, Jefferson, who had returned from Paris to take over as secretary of state, countered that any such idea would violate the doctrine of limited powers that was at the Constitution's core. If Congress was empowered "to do whatever would be good for the United States," then it "would be the sole judge of the good or evil" of its actions.[21] Given that concentrated power was inevitably oppressive—as Madison had put it in the *Federalist Papers*, the "accumulation of all powers, legislative, executive, and judiciary, in the same hands ... may be justly pronounced the very definition of tyranny"—then what Hamilton was proposing was no better than what Americans had risen up against in 1776.[22] Nothing was more dangerous, apparently, than a national government intent on governing. Rather than harmony, the upshot was an ideological conflict so fierce that by 1798–9 Hamilton was actively preparing for civil war. Furious over Jefferson and Madison's repeated attempts to block his policies, he welcomed the prospect of an imminent French invasion in which Southern planters would likely emerge as a Napoleonic fifth column as an opportunity to teach Virginia a lesson once and for all by breaking it up "into more manageable jurisdictions."[23] Yet in the end, it was Hamilton's Federalists who were taught a lesson in Jefferson's "Revolution of 1800" and whose power was broken instead.

What happened? In truth, the Constitution that arose out of the Philadelphia Convention in 1787 was more complex and contradictory than Hamilton—or, for that matter, Jefferson and Madison—realized. It did not establish sovereign government, yet it did not establish limited government either. Instead, it created a federal entity that would be forever torn between the two. It encouraged the people to reach out for absolute power and then to draw back whenever it seemed within their grasp. A people perennially poised on the brink of sovereignty but never quite achieving it was one that would remain neurotic and immobilized. The result was a political framework whose purpose was to neutralize democratic power without actually eliminating it.

4

VICTORY THROUGH FAILURE

SO WHAT WAS THE DOCUMENT calling itself "this Constitution for the United States of America"? The plan of government that emerged from the Philadelphia Convention after nearly four months of wrangling consisted of 4,400 words divided into eight sections. It opened with a Preamble elucidating the relationship between the people and their government, and then moved on to a series of seven articles that detailed the functions of Congress, the presidency, the judiciary, and the states; sketched out a process for amending the Constitution and ratifying it, and announced that, if approved, the document as a whole would henceforth serve as "the supreme law of the land." In one respect, the results were modest. Rather than promising to transform the world and everything in it, it merely announced the people's determination to modify one small corner. Instead of indulging in grandiose rhetoric about liberty and the rights of man, it was filled with homely details concerning how the new arrangement was to function. At the same time, though, the document was little short of encyclopedic. The Preamble offered a mini creation myth about how the new order had come into being, while the rest of the text grappled with such time-honored issues as the different types of political power, the nature of political legitimacy, the problem of political change, and the proper relationship of politics to law. In a few short pages, it seemed to cover all the bases, telling Americans everything they needed to know about how their polity had originated, how it would organize itself, and how it would adapt to changing circumstances. From the tiniest neighborhood squabble to the loftiest national controversy, the new plan of government offered a comprehensive framework for the resolution of any and all problems that might arise.

The Constitution's encyclopedic nature was a result of both the Founders' own inclinations and the system of which they were a part. Practical and methodical, the delegates to the Philadelphia Convention knew all too well that their opponents would seize on any weak spot they could find in order to pull apart the entire structure. Like dutiful lawyers, consequently, they set about drawing up a contract between Americans and their government that would be as ironclad as possible. If the Constitution's sweep was encyclopedic, meanwhile, its structure was Euclidean. At a time when the ancient Greek mathematician's prestige was at its peak—Bertrand Russell once described the eighteenth-century doctrine of natural rights as a search for Euclidean rigor in politics[1]—the document sketched out a relationship between politics, law, and society that aimed to be as tight as a geometrical proof. Where the Declaration of Independence had begun with a series of "self-evident" truths, the Constitution presented itself as a series of irreducible postulates. Power that was divided into three parts, political functions that were carefully distributed between the federal government and the states, an amending clause that was neither too tough nor too easy—the people who had devised the Constitution regarded such principles as equally self-evident truths of good government and hoped that the rest of the population would agree.

If the axioms were right, then the system that flowed from

them would be right also, provided, of course, that the axioms were honestly interpreted and correctly applied. But as sensible as such an approach seemed, it was problematic in a way that few people at the time realized. The reason had to do with the nature of an axiom in a Euclidean system. Once accepted, an axiom or set of axioms must be closed off to further inquiry as long as the larger system continues to function. They must be accepted as "givens," which is to say beyond question. While a Euclidean system invites the invention and discovery of new theorems arising from a given set of postulates, therefore, it simultaneously shuts down any effort to question the postulates themselves. The more it expands, the more thoroughly it must place them off-limits.

The consequences were politically debilitating. If American patriots were to be loyal to the new republic they had helped to create, for example, they had to be loyal to the Declaration of Independence that had given it birth. This meant accepting the proposition that "all men are created equal" as axiomatic, which meant *not* asking how such a thing could be the case when roughly a fifth of the US population in the late eighteenth century were held in slavery. If they were to remain loyal to the new constitutional order, similarly, American patriots would have to banish all questions having to do with the nature of government, the relationship between law and politics, the role of the people, and the purpose of a constitution itself, questions that the Constitution had supposedly settled and questions that would therefore have to remain settled for as long as the Constitution stayed in effect.

This was the original closing of the American mind. Beginning in the 1790s, what we hear from a string of foreign visitors is a series of reports concerning the self-contained nature of the new political culture. As one such visitor, the Duc de Liancourt, observed,

Americans were now convinced "that nothing good is done, and that no one has any brains, except in America; that the wit, the imagination, the genius of Europe are already in decrepitude." In 1796, the House of Representatives seriously debated whether to declare the United States "the freest and most enlightened [nation] in the world"—this at a time, as Henry Adams acidly observed, when the US was "as yet in swaddling-clothes … [with] neither literature, arts, sciences, nor history; nor even enough nationality to be sure it was a nation." In Europe, "Goethe and Schiller, Mozart and Haydn, Kant and Fichte, Cavendish and Herschel were making way for Walter Scott, Wordsworth, and Shelley, Heine and Balzac, Beethoven and Hegel," yet Americans had no use for any of them.[2] Their Constitution held the answer to all questions. As Bill Clinton would later assert: "There's nothing wrong with America that can't be cured by what's right with America"—meaning that there was no reason for America to look outside itself for answers to what lay within.[3]

The Constitution's completeness, its self-sufficient nature, its implicit claim to offer a framework for the resolution of any and all questions that might arise—this was its defining characteristic. The Founders had labored to make the finished product as complete as possible so that ratification would be assured. But once ratification had been achieved, that same completeness served to enclose the polity in a cage of its own making. The Founders sought to limit debate by situating it within a framework based on consensus, compromise, and natural law. But rather than reducing conflict, the ironclad constitutional system compressed and intensified it to the point of explosion.

ONE REASON HAD TO DO with the age-old problem of interpretation. To submit to the Constitution was to submit to the idea that the Constitution should serve as "the supreme law of the land." But while virtually all Americans agreed with this in principle, they disagreed as to what the law actually said. This was especially the case in the ante-bellum period when the Supreme Court had not yet achieved its later lofty status and every citizen claimed the sovereign right to read and interpret the document on his own. In the absence of a single over-arching authority, the result was a legalistic Babel that was impossible to control. Were the people sovereign collectively or individually within the separate states? Did the "necessary and proper" clause allow the federal government to override state prerogatives in order to insure domestic tranquility, or did the concept of delineated powers require it to keep its hands off? Was the Constitution supreme vis-à-vis secular law only or moral law as well? In Federalist No. 10, probably the most famous of the *Federalist Papers*, Madison had argued that while "factious leaders may kindle a flame in their particular States," the proposed new Constitution would insure that they would be "unable to spread a general conflagration" throughout the republic as a whole by dividing power into a multitude of separate categories.[4] Yet the opposite was the case. Thanks to the supremacy clause, the Constit-ution was now the Holy Grail of American politics. Whoever captured "the supreme law of the land" for his side would win. American politics consequently turned into a long-running struggle over interpretation, the purpose of which was to "prove" that the sacred text supported one point of view and not another. Rather than allowing conflict to burn itself out at the local level, the effect was to nation-alize it. "Textualizing" politics meant that anyone who cared about the text would feel obliged to pitch in. Given the text's all-important role throughout US society, few Americans could afford not to.

The Constitution democratized politics while at the same time depriving the demos of the power it needed to resolve political disputes. There is no better example of this process than secession.

Contrary to generations of liberal historians, secession was not some heresy that burst onto the scene in the 1850s, but, rather, a well-established strain of constitutional thought present from the beginning. In arguing that the states served as an essential check on federal power in the famous Virginia and Kentucky Resolutions of 1798, for instance, Jefferson and Madison implied that the states retained the power to withdraw from the Union if their efforts at reining in federal power proved unavailing. Although the Federalists pronounced themselves duly shocked, New Englanders threatened secession in response to the Louisiana Purchase in 1803; to Jefferson's embargo on foreign trade in 1807; and again in response to the War of 1812. Three or four decades later, abolitionists were calling on the North to secede from a Union dominated by slaveholders, while slaveholders were calling on the South to secede from a Union dominated by abolitionists.

Secessionism was a constitutional theory that would not go away because there was no force capable of making it go away. Although the Founders thought they had battened down all hatches, this was one they had left wide open, i.e. the question of whether the United States was a perpetual union or a voluntary experiment from which the individual participants were free to withdraw. For those who agreed with Chief Justice John Marshall that the states had relinquished at least a portion of their sovereignty in joining the new Union back in 1787–8 (even though sovereignty is by definition indivisible), it was plain the states could not take back their full sovereignty unless the Union itself gave its consent. For those who argued that no such surrender had taken place and that the purpose of the federal government was merely to enhance state sovereignty, it was equally plain that the states were free to go their own way. Nationalists could point to the Preamble's injunction "to form a more perfect Union" as proof that the people were only empowered to make the

Union better and not tear it up. But anti-nationalists could point to the Tenth Amendment, which declared that "powers not delegated to the United States by the Constitution, nor prohibited by it to the States, are reserved to the States respectively, or to the people," as evidence that the states were free to do whatever the Constitution did not expressly forbid. In establishing an essentially voluntary relationship between the federal government and the states, they insisted, the Constitution protected the right of the states to withdraw from the federation once they had concluded that it was no longer "secur[ing] the Blessings of Liberty" for themselves and their posterity.

Which interpretation was correct? The question only made sense if one assumed that the Constitution was a coherent document that spoke with a single voice and hence lent itself to a single interpretation. But any such assumption was unwarranted. With its many compromises, the Constitution was in fact an attempt to accommodate many voices whose integration remained incomplete. It was a fundamentally incoherent document that drew those seeking correct, definitive answers deeper and deeper into a labyrinth. The more they searched for meaning, the more it exceeded their grasp.

Indeed, it was precisely this indeterminate quality that ended up pushing both sides in an ever more radical direction. Lincoln, for instance, originally relied on the legalistic argument that because the states had declared independence as the United States of America, they owed their very existence to the Union and therefore could not go their own way without the Union's permission. They could not exercise sovereignty because sovereignty had never been theirs to begin with. Yet once the war was underway, the emphasis in the Republican camp began to shift from what the Founders had done in the eighteenth century to what a sovereign people were doing today. As late as December 1861—seven months into the war—Lincoln told Congress that he was still determined that the conflict not degenerate into "a violent and remorseless revolutionary struggle." A few weeks later, though, George W. Julian, a Radical Republican from Ohio, sounded very much like a Midwestern Robespierre in telling the House:

> Should both Congress and the courts stand in the way of the nation's life, then "the red lightning of the people's wrath" must consume the recreant men who refuse to exercise the people's will. Our country, united and free, must be saved at whatever hazard or cost; and nothing, not even the Constitution, must be allowed to hold back the uplifted arm of the government in blasting the power of the rebels forever.[5]

This was a new kind of popular power—new, at least, as far as the US was concerned—one that was over the Constitution rather than under it. Where the Constitution was the supreme law of the land, the people now exercised "irresistible, absolute, uncontrolled authority" that was supreme over the law. Rather than deriving their authority from something outside themselves, they were their own source. When the New Jersey state legislature dismayed Unionists by calling for a negotiated settlement in early 1863, members of the Eleventh New Jersey Regiment responded in a manner that was similarly unqualified. Denouncing the state legislature as "wicked, weak, and cowardly," they vowed that "every armed rebel shall be conquered, and traitors at home shall quake with fear, as the proud emblem of our national independence shall assert its power from North to South, and crush beneath its powerful folds all who dared to assail its honor...."[6] Rather than dividing power into separate channels designed to limit one another's power, the people were concentrating it in preparation for the final assault.

Lincoln's Gettysburg Address, delivered in November 1863, further reflected this shift. The famous opening reference to events "four score and seven years ago" was a nod to the old argument that the Union of 1776 was still superior over the individual states. But in the very next sentence, Lincoln abandoned the past in order better to concentrate on the here-and-now. "The world will little note nor long remember what we say here," he declared, "but it can never forget what they did here." Rather than blindly adhering to precedent, Union soldiers were creating new precedents that others were morally obliged to follow. Instead of restoring the *status quo ante*, it was up to "us the living" to create "a new birth of freedom" that would be better than what had preceded it. Rather than a system of checks and balances and limited power government that implied a wary, arm's-length relationship between the people and their government, the goal now was nothing less than "government of the people, by the people, for the people," which is to say government that incorporated the popular will so completely that it and people were one and the same. The fixed and static rules of eighteenth-century republicanism had given way to a new concept of a people's government in which the only mandate was to do whatever the people wished.

Or had they? Lincoln's problem is that he wanted to have it both ways, to base his actions on the Founders while at the same time calling for "a new birth of freedom" that was different from what the Founders had created. But if the United States had indeed been "conceived in liberty and dedicated to the proposition that all men are created equal," why was a new birth necessary in the first place? Was the old freedom in some way inadequate or incomplete? In fact, any number of discordant elements had gone into the making of the original revolution—planters, artisans, bourgeois, and so forth—and now, after some seventy years of rising tension, they were finally sorting things out. If the struggle for independence had corresponded to the Girondist, or moderate, phase of the French Revolution, then the Civil War corresponded to its Jacobin second act. But where the French could still discuss events in their own country with a degree of frankness, Americans could not. The cult of the Constitution prevented anything by way of penetrating analysis. Instead of declaring that the old republic had been fundamentally flawed, it required that Americans still pay obeisance to the debilitating myth that the US had been perfect in the past and would be even more perfect in the years to come.

This explains why American revolutionary energies vanished so completely once the emergency had passed. In the course of the war, the people had come close to establishing themselves as an independent force over and above the Constitution. They had shown their determination to preserve the nation, "united and free," at whatever cost. In the final analysis, though, notwithstanding the neo-Jacobin rhetoric of people like George W. Julian, they never reached the point of overthrowing shibboleths dating from the previous century. As the Yale constitutional scholar Bruce Ackerman has noted, Americans might very well have seized the opportunity to draft a new constitution beginning with the words, "We the People of the United States, in order to form a more perfect Union after the terrible ordeal of Civil War, do ordain this Constitution...."[7] Other countries had done the same under similar circumstances, so why not the US? But instead of reconstitution, Congress opted for a lesser policy of reconstruction based on the fiction that secession had been exclusively a Southern malady that would go away as soon as the South was reformed. As a result, Congress deliberately avoided the question of how secession had arisen out of the Union as a whole. Deploying troops to protect ex-slaves was no substitute for mobilizing the people in general in order to reshape the entire political system.

The impeachment of Andrew Johnson in 1868 might conceivably have been the constitutional event that forced Americans to jettison their ties with the past. Had it been successful, it would likely have marked the beginning of the end not only of an independent presidency, but of separation of powers, checks and balances, and other relics of the sixteenth century. As a conservative but none the less astute *Harper's Weekly* noted, impeachment would have "become an ordinary party measure" if Johnson had been convicted, the independence of the executive branch would have been "destroyed" and "the balance of the whole system [would have come] to an end."[8] After taking such a momentous step, Congress, not unlike parliament in the 1640s, would have had no choice but to develop new modes of government to deal with new circumstances. The fact that impeachment did not end in conviction—Johnson was acquitted by a single vote—meant that Congress was off the hook, free to return to its old ways of doing business.

Of course, a young Woodrow Wilson would subsequently complain that Congress was already too powerful relative to the other branches. But the congressional dominance that Wilson criticized in the 1870s was of a different sort. Instead of forging new paths, the legislative branch was sinking back into its old lethargy and taking the rest of the system with it. Congressional dominance now meant the dominance of the old clubhouse politics, the smoke-filled room, and the backroom deal. The staggering growth of corruption and plutocracy during this period was the result of deepening constitutional stagnation, as was the growing wave of anti-labor violence, an area in which America's lead was even more impressive than in the production of wheat or steel. Where seven workers were killed in labor disputes in Britain between 1872 and 1914, sixteen were killed in Germany, and thirty-five were killed in France, the same period saw at least 500 to 800 deaths in the United States. Only Czarist Russia had a bloodier record.[9] A worker who dared to go on strike in Illinois was ten times likelier to be arrested for his efforts than a worker in France.[10] Although only one of two republics in the advanced industrial world as of the 1870s, America was increasingly a republic of wealth rather than people. Democratic standards were plunging below those of Northern Europe, which is one reason why immigration from that region was rapidly tailing off.

WAS THE CONSTITUTION A SUCCESS or failure? Ultimately, the question is one of perspective. From a democratic point of view, it thoroughly flunked the great test of the 1850s and '60s. By entrenching slavery and surrounding it with a series of impregnable defenses, the Constitution prevented the people from abolishing a system that a growing national majority found intolerable and repugnant. Thanks to the three-fifths clause and equal state representation in the Senate, the Constitution exaggerated the slavocracy's clout in both houses of Congress, in the Electoral College, and hence in the presidency and the judiciary. In contrast to the Jeffersonian nightmare of a tyrannical majority, it gave a tyrannical *minority* a degree of control over the federal government that was all but unbreakable. Given slavery's various constitutional protections, the logical thing would have been for the Northern masses to amend the Constitution in order to remove them. Yet the two-thirds/three-fourths rule set forth in Article V prevented them from acting. As long as the South controlled more than a quarter of the states, it could veto any effort aimed at constitutionally dethroning slavery. A people's constitution prevented a popular majority from exercising its will. Unable to resolve the slavery issue constitutionally, the demos had no choice but to resolve it extra-constitutionally via the military. As glorious as the Civil War may have been, it was an example of how the Constitution forced the people to resort to extraordinary measures to accomplish what they should have been able to accomplish through ordinary democratic means.

"The constitutional catastrophe of the Civil War," a legal scholar recently declared, "... was one of the greatest political failures in world history that can be linked to a constitution, perhaps only exceeded by the failure of the Weimar Constitution ... in 1933."[11] But if constitutional failure was a catastrophe for the nation, it was a triumph for the Constitution itself since it allowed it carry on with remarkably little change. In the final analysis, the three Civil War amendments adopted in 1865–70 provided for remarkably little alteration in the status quo. While the Thirteenth Amendment abolished slavery, it did nothing to prevent the Southern Bourbons, successors to the old slavocracy, from forcing blacks into a form of peonage that in some ways was worse than the bondage they had recently escaped. Where the Fourteenth Amendment declared that Southern blacks were entitled to full rights of US citizenship, subsequent judicial rulings whittled down nearly to zero the rights the federal government was obligated to protect. While the Fifteenth Amendment guaranteed that the right to vote would not be abridged "on account of race, color, or previous condition of servitude," it said nothing about economic status, a loophole that allowed the Southern ruling class to curtail the voting privileges of both blacks and poor whites.

The states' rights that a restored Constitution helped re-impose after the war allowed Southern white landowners to once again monopolize power at the state level. If the old three-fifths clause had rewarded slaveholders, as the abolitionist William Lloyd Garrison tirelessly pointed out, then a Jim Crow system that counted blacks as "five-fifths" of a person for purposes of congressional representation while still depriving them of a vote was an even more potent incentive to keep Afro-Americans "in their place." Once it had "allowed" the people to solve the slavery problem in the most minimal fashion, the Constitution returned the country to a condition notably similar in many respects to that which had prevailed before the war. It was able to preserve its integrity by holding back democratic reform. The result for both Southern blacks and impoverished Southern whites was more than a century of constitutionally enforced backwardness and stagnation, while for American workers as a whole the upshot was political corruption and ferocious repression of labor rights.

THE CONSTITUTION'S QUASI-DARWINIAN instinct for survival was evident after the Civil War era. Broadly speaking, the constitutional system can be described as oscillating between repression and accommodation after the crucial turning point of 1876–77, when the Republican government in Washington opted to abandon Southern blacks to their fate in order to devote its resources to battling militant workers in the North. Rather than alternate strategies, however, repression and accommodation should be seen as two sides of the same coin. Just as middle-class Progressives could be no less fierce in combating organized labor than the haute bourgeoisie (in some cases, they could be even fiercer), all but the most obdurate employers recognized that more sophisticated means of persuasion were needed to keep workers in line other than machineguns and bayonets. Where a leading Southern employer declared in the 1890s that "a law should be passed that would make it justifiable homicide for any killing that occurred in defense of any lawful" business, Francis Lynde Stetson, J.P. Morgan's personal attorney, argued in more sophisticated terms in the auspicious year of 1917 that the discontent of the masses "is to be allayed not by a policy of stern and unyielding toryism," but by more flexible social policies.[12]

The goal, none the less, was the same: to accommodate industrial capitalism within the confines of a pre-industrial Constitution. Progressivism sought to neutralize popular political power via such measures as primary elections and nonpartisan municipal government, both based on the notion that concentrated political power was inherently abusive unless carefully controlled, regulated, and broken up by the bourgeois state. For all its fulminations against monopoly capitalism, populism, in the words of the spellbinding orator James H. "Cyclone" Davis, was an attempt to return America to its eighteenth-century roots by sending a message to Thomas Jefferson, "the sainted sire of American liberty, ... that there is another hereditary high-handed aristocracy in our land."[13]

Fordism, the most comprehensive reform movement of them all, was an especially powerful blend of progressivism, populism, and plutocracy. Born and raised a Michigan farm boy, Henry Ford was filled with the characteristic country loathing of the day for cities, Jews, imperialism, militarism, high finance, and big business in general. He conceived of the Model T not just as a means of personal transport, but as an instrument of social change, a means of returning US to a program of Jeffersonian agrarianism. "Amid all the writing now done on efficiency and freedom in politics," he wrote in the *Dearborn Independent*, the country weekly that he used in the 1920s to propagate his increasingly fascistic views, "none is more modern than Jefferson." "America," he added, "is made, not to be remade or unmade, but to go on being made according to the original pattern of a land and a government for all people capable of receiving liberty."[14] This was the old ideology of the Ancient Constitution, a belief system that argued that a nation does not grow by "moving away from an initial starting point," to quote one historian, but instead involved "a process by which an entity (such as a nation) became more itself over time."[15] Since America was conceived in liberty, it would remain a beacon of liberty only to the degree it remained true to its original principles.

Ford was an extreme proponent of both the carrot and the stick—two cars in every garage and the five-dollar-a-day wage in combination with stepped-up violence against leftists and union organizers and with increasing friendliness toward the Third Reich abroad. As such, he was a fascinating example of how the twentieth-century Jeffersonian revival was segueing into Nazism. But the American constitutional dialectic between accommodation and repression also gave rise to the New Deal. Where Fordism had all but economically collapsed in the wake of the Crash of 1929, Roosevelt's aim was to get it going again by broadening its social base and altering the political framework in which it operated. Despite his reputation for pragmatism, FDR was an enthusiastic Jeffersonian who shared fully in Ford's belief that cities had grown too large and had to be cut down to size. Homeownership, suburbanization, and highway construction, consequently, were among the New Deal's top priorities.[16] But where Ford was a ferocious union-buster even by the standards of American big business, Roosevelt's approach was subtler. While the National Labor Relations Act of 1933, a landmark New Deal measure, gave union organizers a degree of legal protection, it simultaneously ensnared them in a dense legal web that over time would grow more and more constricting. Roosevelt's constitutional reforms were equally clever. His first term was dominated by a growing confrontation with a conservative Supreme Court representing all that was most hidebound and obsolete about the American constitutional tradition. Following a short-lived showdown early in his second term, however, he abandoned his feud and embarked instead on a strategy of revolutionizing the court from within by transforming it from a conservative stronghold to a bastion of liberal reform.

THE AUDACITY OF THIS APPROACH cannot be overstated; essentially, it gave us the modern Constitution. Previously, liberals and leftists had scorned the court as a mainstay of constitutional obscurantism. The justices were "nine old men" in FDR's memorable phrase, intent on just saying no to any and all forms of social reform. But once Roosevelt began packing the court with liberals, attitudes did an about-face. Within a few years, Popular Frontists such as Max Lerner had forgotten their bitter criticism of the judicial branch and had reinvented themselves as pious devotees.[17] The Supreme Court guarded the holy text as jealously as ever. It still stood for the elevation of a timeless body of basic law over the democratic will. But because it now did so in the name of reform, liberals pronounced themselves more Catholic than the pope, more dedicated to the rule of law than the most die-hard conservatives. Where conservative jurists had relied on the ancient law as a bulwark against change, liberals now worked overtime transforming it into an agent of modernization.

Liberal constitutionalism became the new orthodoxy. Hamilton had predicted that the judiciary would be "beyond comparison the weakest of the three departments of power," but postwar developments stood that judgment on its head.[18] Beginning in the mid-1950s, the Supreme Court handed down one near-revolutionary ruling after another. The *Brown v. Board of Education* school desegregation ruling in 1954; the *Baker v. Carr* one person-one vote decision in 1962; the 1966 *Miranda* ruling declaring that individuals under arrest were entitled to legal representation; the *Griswold v. Connecticut* decision the same year striking down laws against birth control; the *Roe v. Wade* pro-abortion ruling in 1973—these were just some of the decisions that were transforming American society. Not that the court's power should be exaggerated: if hadn't been for the courage of thousands of civil rights workers plus the growing militancy of the Northern black masses, desegregation would have proceeded at a snail's pace. Still, the court's role was indisputable. Not only did it provide the civil rights movement with a mantle of constitutional legitimacy, it provided the constitutional system with a mantle of moral legitimacy it had previously lacked. A system that had seemed tired and played out as recently as the 1930s now seemed fresh and reinvigorated. "If we are wrong," King told his followers in 1955, "then the Supreme Court of this nation is wrong. If we are wrong, the Constitution of the United States is wrong. If we are wrong, God Almighty is wrong."[19] Since King and his followers were obviously right in liberal eyes, then God, the Constitution, and the Supreme Court were right also. As Gunnar Myrdal once observed, America is never more conservative than when it is at its most liberal.[20]

American constitutionalism was a zero-sum game. In order to go forward in one area, liberals felt obliged to go back in another. If they were to use the Constitution to advance the cause of black equality, they felt that, pragmatically, their only choice was to propagate an essentially mystical view of the document as simultaneously ancient and modern, timeless yet timely as an instrument of legal reform. Madison and Jefferson had both owned slaves. For decades prior to the 1860s, the Constitution they helped create had strengthened slavery by giving Southern planters an effective veto over the democratic majority. For nearly a century after the Civil War, it had allowed them to subject black people to an unremitting reign of terror. But now the same Madisonian system was setting them free. The Constitution was the all-powerful enslaver and liberator, an instrument of oppression and a beacon of hope for the oppressed. Depending on how it was interpreted, it could be anything and its opposite, which is why the struggle for control of the Supreme Court, guardian of the sacred text, grew ever more urgent.

But were pragmatists correct in arguing that the Constitution is infinitely malleable? It was one thing to say that as a bundle of contradictions, the document could be interpreted in a variety of ways. But the Constitution structured American politics and intellectual life by virtue of its contradictions. By being of two minds concerning popular sovereignty—hinting at it in the Preamble, rejecting it in Article V—it insured that American politics would forever oscillate back and forth between the two positions. By imposing a set of static supra-political values on society, it wound up freezing politics in place. Regardless of what argument he or she was making, every constitutional lawyer who appeared before the Supreme Court helped strengthen this paralyzing constitutional orthodoxy. By basing their argument on a close reading of the sacred text, they wound up reinforcing the view that the Founders' teachings were "controlling." The inability to argue such questions on the basis of modern democratic theory rather than eighteenth-century republicanism was an indication of their obeisance to the past.

Indeed, by the 1950s, a new dialectic was at work. The more liberal reform was "constitutionalized," the more liberal politics were enfeebled. The more liberals celebrated the Supreme Court, the more they accepted it as a given that the elected branches were hopeless. The House was gridlocked, senators were too busy racing from fundraiser to fundraiser, while the president couldn't choose a tie without checking with his pollsters—given all this, what was a liberal reformer to do other than to file another legal brief? The more dependent liberalism grew on the courts, the more it defined itself in terms of its eagerness to obey this or that judicial pronouncement. Popular sovereignty in the liberal imagination became synonymous with white homeowners in Cicero, Illinois, snarling obscenities at Martin Luther King, just as in the 1850s it was synonymous with Southern partisans trying to secure Kansas's entry into the Union as a slave state. Popular sovereignty was indistinguishable from mob rule. Instead of freeing the people to alter their political environment as they might wish, the new goal was to create a Madisonian zone of freedom by hemming in popular politics on every side with judicial decisions and the rule of law.

WATERGATE WAS A HIGH-WATER MARK for such attitudes. If the US Civil War of 1861–65 were a replay to a degree of the English Civil War of the 1640s, the events of 1972–74 were a remarkably faithful replay of the Glorious Revolution of 1688–89 when parliament forced out yet another overweening Stuart. In both instances, the problem was that of an out-of-control chief executive, James II on one hand, Richard Nixon on the other. Rather than simply doing away with the crown, members of the patriotic opposition insisted that they wanted nothing more than for the chief executive to abide by the Ancient Constitution. Parliament insisted that it had not forced James II to give up the throne and flee to France, but, in accordance with established law, had merely brought in a new team, the dual monarchy of William and Mary, to take over a throne that he had inexplicably deserted. Equally anxious not to be seen as forcing Nixon out of office, Congress insisted that it merely wanted him to comply with established law by turning over certain White House tapes as the Supreme Court had ordered.

In both cases, legislators portrayed themselves as servants rather than masters of the law. As Barbara Jordan, a black Democratic congresswoman from Texas, declared as Watergate was nearing its finale: "My faith in the Constitution is whole, it is complete, it is total, and I am not going to sit here and be an idle spectator to the diminution, the subversion, the destruction of the Constitution." The Constitution was Congress's sword and shield. If the executive would not defer to the majesty of law, then, however reluctantly, the legislative branch would have no choice but to bring in someone who would.

Despite their liberal veneer, both events were constitutionally conservative. In 1688, Edmund Ludlow, an unrepentant old Puritan who was among those who had condemned Charles I to death in 1649, hurried home from his place of exile to what he assumed would be a hero's welcome on the part of a new generation of revolutionaries. Instead, parliament sent him packing. Rather than revolution, what conservative MPs wanted was law and order and constitutional stability. In a similar spirit, the *Washington Post* sent two of its top editors into the streets the day Nixon resigned looking for signs of unrest. Happily, they reported back that everything was under control:

> There was no chorus of jubilation in Washington and no cries for vengeance and retribution. There was an absence of turmoil, mobs, violence, massive protests. The crowds that began gathering at the White House on Tuesday remained quiet, solemn and patient. They were witnesses to history, yes, and someday they would tell their grandchildren about it. But now ... they seemed more preoccupied by personal feelings of sorrow and sadness.[21]

Rather than actors, the people were no more than spectators, silent witnesses to history. Given the Constitution's triumph over popular sovereignty, all it allowed them to do was stand by and watch. The king had been overthrown so that the old order could be restored.

5

THE LONG GOODBYE

IN THE AFTERMATH of the Watergate crisis, Barbara Jordan's impassioned remarks were broadcast over and over again on TV. Everything about her performance was impressive, her dignity, her refined diction, her vaguely professorial demeanor. As a black woman from the Deep South, she was a member of an outcast race who, against all odds, had carved out a distinguished career for herself and was now stepping forward to save the republic at the moment of its greatest peril. For many Americans, her sound bite was the defining moment of the anti-Nixonian resistance, a *cri de coeur* that summed up the republic at its bravest, most principled, and most inclusive.

But did Americans actually *think* about what Jordan was saying? Judging from the giddy press coverage, the answer is no. If they had, they might have been slightly less swept away. After all, what did it mean to express complete and unqualified approval of a document as lengthy and complex as the US Constitution? What could Jordan have meant in saying that her faith "is whole, it is complete, it is total"? Was it whole, complete, and total in the three-fifths clause and other provisions that had protected slavery for more than seven decades? Was it whole, complete, and total in a Senate that flouts the principle of one person-one vote in granting equal representation to a multi-racial giant like California and a lily-white rotten borough like Wyoming even though the latter's population is more than ninety-eight percent smaller? Was it whole, etc., in an Electoral College that, by awarding votes on the basis of a state's total number of senators and representatives, gives voters in the smallest states three times as much clout in presidential elections? Was it whole in an amending clause that allows thirteen states representing as little as five percent of the US population to block constitutional reforms sought by the other ninety-five percent? Considering that the very existence of an amending clause is an admission that the Constitution may require fixing from time to time, how could one express perfect faith in a document that is imperfect by its own admission?

It was a bit like the words of the Holy Mass: the more one thought about them, the more paradoxical they became. US politics emerged triumphant from Watergate for all the wrong reasons: not because Americans had wrestled with the ideas underlying their government and given thought to how they might be improved, but because they had once again gotten away with relying on the wisdom of the ancients. "The system worked," to quote the mantra of the day, meaning that the people could go back to sleep while politics continued on autopilot. Post-Nixon, reinvigorated separation of powers led to deepening gridlock on Capitol Hill, which helped make a shambles of the Carter administration and clear the way for Ronald Reagan in 1980. The Iran–contra affair, the climax of half a dozen years of deadly dueling over policy in Central America, was in some respects a replay of Watergate, but many times more serious. Instead of a dirty-tricks squad composed of over-the-hill intelligence agents, it featured a concerted effort by top Reagan officials to circumvent congressional control in order to funnel aid to rightwing Nicaraguan terrorists. Yet Congress's performance a second time around couldn't have been feebler. Rather than reining in a runaway White House, the people's representatives listened meekly as a defiant marine colonel named Oliver North told them that they could not be trusted with sensitive information because they were weak and undisciplined. In a particularly telling moment, North, after inflicting his tongue-lashing, stepped out in full dress uniform onto the balcony of a federal office building at the end of the day to wave, Juan Peron-style, to the cheering throngs below.

This is the way democracies die, not with a bang, but with a whimper on the part of legislators who have lost both their nerve and their capacity for independent thought. Iran–contra gave way to the budget paralysis of the Bush years, a near-mutiny in the Pentagon over the issue of gays in the military, back-to-back government shutdowns in early 1996, and seemingly endless investigations of the Clinton administration by no fewer than seven independent prosecutors. By the time impeachment came along in 1998, Congress was seething with revolt and filled with would-be Barbara Jordans spouting consti-tutional platitudes and hoping for their fifteen minutes of fame. It wasn't partisan politics, they insisted, that sent them chasing after a mildly liberal president like so many attack dogs. Rather, it was the Constitution, that noble fabric, the pride of America, the envy of her neighbors, raised by the labor of so many centuries, and so forth, as Bolingbroke would no doubt have put it had he been a member of the Grand Old Party. "The Constitution provides a path to follow in these circumstances," Asa Hutchinson, an Arkansas Republican, declared during the House impeachment debate. "The path may be well worn, but it is well marked, and we would be wise to follow it, rather than concoct our own theories on how to proceed." Not to be outdone, Zoe Lofgren, a California Democrat, gushed: "When we are lost, the best

THE VELVET COUP

thing to do is to look to our Constitution as a beacon of light and a guide to get us through trying times."[1] Thinking for oneself was dangerous. Trusting in the sacred wisdom of the Founders was by far the safer course. Liberty depended on fidelity to an ancient body of law regardless of what the ancient law might be.

And ancient it was. Derived from the Middle French verb *empecher*, to catch, impeachment dates from the mid-fourteenth century when parliament still thought of itself as a court whose job was to apply existing law rather than a legislative body creating new law to fit new circumstances. At a time when the English throne was unusually powerful in comparison with other European monarchies, impeachment represented a pioneering effort on the part of parliament to exert control over the executive branch.[2] Even by medieval standards, however, using criminal law in this way was clumsy and inefficient, which is why impeachment fell into disuse in the fifteenth century, then again in the seventeenth century following a short-lived revival, and all but disappeared, finally, in the late 1700s. Parliament had tested it and found it wanting. No longer content merely to check royal power, it had begun the long process of assuming executive functions directly. Yet the delegates to the Constitutional Convention, unfamiliar with the real state of British government, took a relic of Anglo-Norman law that was headed for oblivion and made it a major instrument of congressional control. Conceivably, Congress might have used impeachment for progressive purposes in 1868, but that was far from the case in the waning days of the twentieth century. The instrument's archaic nature determined the ends to which it would be put. Whatever Clinton's faults, impeachment was bound to degenerate into a neo-medieval witch-hunt in pursuit of semen-stained dresses and fellatio in the Oval Office.

Not that Clinton's outlook was fundamentally more modern. As the wily ex-governor of a Southern state, Clinton was also fond of spouting constitutional clichés whenever he thought it would suit his purposes. Introducing Supreme Court nominee Stephen G. Breyer to the press in 1994, he said of Breyer: "You know, this country got started by people who wanted a good letting alone from government. I think he understands that."[3] This would no doubt have come as a surprise to the New England Puritans, a people who never left anyone alone about anything. But the comment allowed Clinton to waft a carefully crafted message in the direction of Capitol Hill, one that promised Republicans that Breyer would not be the sort of judicial activist who would cause them to lose sleep while offering equal assurances to Democrats that he would vigorously protect privacy rights.

It was an example of the studied ambiguity that is at the heart of American political rhetoric. But Clinton's comments sent another message as well. The sentence, "I think he understands that," was also double-edged. On one hand, it implied that Breyer was knowledgeable about the historical forces that had shaped American development. On the other, it implied that the nominee was not only historically well versed, but that he recognized that original patterns of development must continue. It implied that Breyer understood that the founding generation's original intent must still to be regarded as paramount. While Republicans and Democrats might argue over exactly what that original intent might be, the game of American politics required that both sides claim to be merely executing the will of a group of eighteenth-century tribal patriarchs. While Americans were free to interpret the Founders' words as they wished, they were not free to disregard them. In order to win, they had to paint themselves as truer to the past than their opponents.

CLINTON WAS THE ARTFUL DODGER, skilled in the use of Country-style rhetoric to confuse his enemies and keep his administration afloat. Yet under his reign, the crisis of American politics continued to accelerate. Personally liberal, with a weakness for pizza, cigars, and *zoftig* White House interns, Clinton none the less presided over a period of rising repression and inequality. During his first term in office, drug arrests in the United States rose forty-four percent to 1.53 million a year. Although a 1998 federal survey showed that five times as many whites use illegal drugs, blacks were five times likelier to be arrested on a drug rap during his administration and better than thirteen times likelier to be sent to prison. "We really need an examination of our entire prison policy," Clinton told *Rolling Stone* magazine as his term in office was drawing to a close. Yet the US incarceration rate during his reign rose thirty-six percent to 690 per 100,000 people, the highest in the world, while the total population under the control of the American penal system (i.e. behind bars, on probation, or on parole) reached 6.5 million.[4] Clinton also presided over a tripling of America's capital punishment rate to one execution nearly every four days.[5] Along with Iran, Pakistan, and Saudi Arabia, the US was just one of a half-dozen nations that still put felons to death for crimes committed under the age of eighteen.

Thanks to its eighteenth-century Constitution, America was circling back to an eighteenth-century code of justice in which judges in horsehair wigs declared that morality would crumble if they didn't sentence twelve-year-old pickpockets to the gibbet. Clinton also presided over a period of increasingly poisonous political relations on Capitol Hill. Not that this was his fault, of course, but still he was powerless to stop it. Although political commentators in the 1980s and '90s repeatedly predicted the demise of American conservatism, the right wing emerged from one crisis after another bloodier but still unbowed. Iran–contra, George Bush's embarrassing retreat from his 1988 "no new taxes" pledge, the back-to-back resignations of House Speaker Newt Gingrich and Speaker-designate Robert Livingston due to sexual improprieties—none of it mattered. Rather than sapping the right's self-confidence, such incidents emboldened it. The growing influence of Christian fundamentalism was particularly striking. Hard as it is to imagine in the opening years of the twenty-first century, the Christian right's hold on the Reagan administration was never more than slight. Reagan rarely indulged in religious displays, while issues like school prayer were far from the grand obsessions they would eventually become. Yet religious fundamentalism expanded so dramatically after Reagan that the 2000 presidential election featured not one but two born-again candidates: "Dubya," who described Christ as his favorite philosopher and had once signed a proclamation declaring an annual "Jesus Day" in Texas, and Al Gore, who informed voters that the number one question on his mind at all times was "WWJD"— "What would Jesus do?"[6] Indeed, it was not a Republican but a Democrat, vice presidential candidate Joe Lieberman, who declared during the campaign that "the Constitution guarantees freedom *of* religion, not freedom *from* religion," implying that Americans enjoyed no constitutional right to disbelieve.[7]

Rather than exclusively the fault of the GOP, America's race to the right was a function of the larger political system. Despite efforts to recast the Constitution as an instrument of modernization and reform, the very idea of an unchangeable plan of government resting on unchallengeable eighteenth-century beliefs was a powerful conservative influence. By making *stare decisis*, the notion that precedent rules, the dominant principle among both liberals and conservatives, it tethered the US to the pre-industrial past and led to repeated spiritual crises whenever the polity seemed in danger of pulling away. As

Michael Hardt and Antonio Negri point out in a recent study of American foreign policy, the Founders' goal was to create unity out of discord by using the conflicts among the various constituent elements to create a harmonious whole. The equilibrium that would result when the different branches were all neatly balanced against one another would serve as an index of republican virtue since it would mean that each political actor was fulfilling his time-honored role with proper patriotic zeal. "Any disequilibrium among these powers," Hardt and Negri add, would likewise be seen as "a symptom of corruption" since it would mean that at least some of the players were neglecting their duties.[8] But the problem with this formula is the problem of capitalism itself. Because it is inherently destabilizing, capitalism continually upsets the balance of power. It throws the system out of kilter in a way that the system is programmed to interpret as indicative of corruption, subversion, and decay. The upshot is periodic attempts to undo subversion and decay by driving the modernizers out of the temple, scrubbing the altar clean, and restoring the Founders' teachings to their rightful place of honor. The older and more attenuated such a system becomes, the more feverish such efforts grow. Regeneration is increasingly defined as a process by which unbelievers are cast out so that the republic can once again establish itself as a community of faith.

This explains America's growing religiosity, its nostalgia for the patriotic 1940s and '50s (evident in such exercises in mass sentimentality as the 1998 Steven Spielberg film *Saving Private Ryan*), and its increasingly cloying political rhetoric. Skepticism must be banished, it seems, so that Americans can once again believe. They must believe in America in order to believe in themselves, and vice versa. It also explains why calls to "take back America" have grown increasingly common from the 1970s on. If American society seems more and more dysfunctional, then it must be the fault of various unpatriotic elements who have hijacked the ancient republic and diverted it from its true path. Restoring the republic to good health meant wresting it away from "miners and sappers" (in Jefferson's famous phrase) who have infiltrated its defenses and returning it to ancient ways.

ULTIMATELY, OF COURSE, this rightwing trend is a consequence of a global capitalist downturn that began in the early 1970s and continued to gain force in the following decades.[9] But it would be sterile and unproductive to suggest that the Kondratieff long wave is all that matters and that the question of political structure can be safely ignored. To the contrary, it is the interaction of economics and politics that by the 1980s and '90s was leading to a growing constitutional crisis not only in all three branches of government, but at all three levels (i.e. federal, state, and local), and in the political parties as well.

Consider, for example, the problem of gridlock and the decline of a two-party system that by now is nearly a century-and-a-half old. The Founders viewed party politics with typical eighteenth-century disdain as representing the triumph of private over public interests. High-minded statesmen avoided such backroom cabals like the plague, which is why Washington was careful to keep himself aloof from the bitter ideological disputes that were wracking his administration by the early 1790s. At the same time, though, the new system encouraged political parties by opening the door to mass politics, if only a crack. By the 1830s, a form of government designed in opposition to the very idea of party politics had thus given rise to the first modern party system. At a time when the Whigs and Tories were little more than parliamentary factions, American parties were whipping up voters with a highly theatrical form of outdoor politics complete with stump speeches, torchlight parades, slogans, and jingles.

This is an irony worth savoring. But if the American system raised the party to one level of development, it was unable to raise it to the next level, that of the party as the expression of a self-governing mass movement. This was a form that European social democrats would pioneer in the 1870s and that bourgeois movements would soon emulate. Rather than drumming up passing enthusiasm for this or that favorite son, this new type of organization organized the people into a disciplined, dues-paying force. In contrast to the American concept of the party platform as so much window dressing that politicians were free to ignore, it ran candidates solely for the purpose of implementing an ongoing program of comprehensive political change. Parties like these (at least those on the left) were not content merely to coordinate policy between and among the various branches of government; their goal, rather, was to transform themselves, their followers, and the political systems of which they were a part. Representative democracy, based on the individual representation of specific interests, lost ground to a new concept of mass democracy in which parties governed directly as the expression of class forces. Where an eighteenth-century gentleman believed it would be corrupt to subordinate himself to party dictates, a new generation of party activists held that it would be corrupt not to.

Yet America was never able to move beyond the old Jeffersonian-Jacksonian model. The reasons were many: an ultra-fragmented political structure, institutionalized parochialism, but most of all a constitutional structure that subordinated politics to a permanent body of basic law and therefore fairly banished the idea of a single party transforming the whole of society. Rather than taking the Constitution in hand, the parties placed themselves under its wing, thoroughly absorbing its values. They functioned as "big tent" federations, capable of saying one thing in one part of the country and the opposite in another, as Democratic support for racial integration in the North and Jim Crow in the South well into the 1960s illustrated. Prevented from growing, the party system rapidly deteriorated. By 1946, a study by the American Political Science Association found that the two major parties had not substantially changed from pre-Civil War days, that they were more concerned with state and local issues than national affairs, that their membership was fast becoming irrelevant, and that special interest groups and lobbying organizations were rapidly supplanting their roles.[10] Yet a series of misguided liberal reforms in the 1950s and '60s only made matters worse. The primary system, which gained speed after the disastrous Democratic National Convention of 1968, took a closed-door nomination process involving a handful of kingmakers and replaced it with a chaotic free-for-all in which individual candidates race from one state contest to another with a small army of pollsters, campaign consultants, media experts, and journalists in tow. Post-Watergate spending reform turned individual candidates into lone-wolf entrepreneurs chasing after corporate contributions to fuel their increasingly expensive campaigns. Instead of seeking political support, candidates now test-marketed slogans to see which would "sell" to a jaded public. Political ads became indistinguishable from commercials for laundry detergent, peanut butter, and other artifacts of an overstuffed consumer economy.

In their prime, the parties had imposed a degree of consistency on a deliberately ramshackle system of government in which inconsistency was seen as a virtue. But as party discipline declined, inter-branch coordination declined with it. Divided government, in which Democrats and Republicans split control of the elected branches, had been the exception in the first half of the twentieth century, but after 1952 it became the rule two times out of three. By

1990, sixty-seven percent of the American electorate were telling pollsters that they preferred to split up political power rather than allowing one party to control the House, Senate, and presidency. Pundits and academics moaned that such attitudes were self-defeating. By dividing control in such a manner, voters were merely ensuring that government would wind up more confused than ever. But while criticism of this sort was not incorrect, it failed to take into account the logic imposed by the larger Madisonian system. If checks and balances were good, voters figured that the added check that would come from placing each branch in separate party hands was even better.[11] Rather than "throwing the bastards out," the idea now seemed to be to throw both sets of bastards in so that they could better serve as "spies or checks upon one another."

Gridlock and decay did not affect the two parties equally. Once they had recovered from the debacle of Watergate, Republicans proved more successful in holding their troops together and hammering out a consistent program. For most of the twentieth century, the intelligentsia had been firmly Democratic. Yet by the 1970s, the GOP was able to begin assembling a formidable intellectual apparatus of its own, one composed of think-tank conservatives, free-market economists, and right-wing pundits in the broadcast and print media. By the early 1990s, media saturation reached the point where it seemed all but impossible to turn on cable-TV news or a radio talk show without being assaulted by some *enragée* of the right denouncing "feminazis" or the plague of "political correctness." The GOP was not without its setbacks. Newt Gingrich's 1994 Contract With America, for example, seemed at the point of revolutionizing American politics by equipping the GOP with a genuine party program that Republican congressional candidates were committed to implementing. Yet on closer analysis, the contract turned out to be a grab bag of half-baked ideas that Gingrich had cooked up with his cronies in Gopac, his personal campaign vehicle, as a PR stunt and then foisted on his fellow Republicans.[12] Once elected, GOP members of the House began backing away, and little of it, in fact, became law. In the end, Gingrich's confrontational tactics helped pave the way for Clinton's decisive re-election victory in 1996.

Still, the prevailing capitalist winds were in the Republicans' favor, while the Democrats seemed increasingly at a loss. The welfare state that the party had cobbled together in the 1960s (with GOP acquiescence) was a mess, an ad-hoc effort at buying social peace by throwing benefits at urban politicians who had previously been shut out of the scramble. Rather than doing away with pork-barrel corruption, it expanded it, which is why Democrats quickly retreated once conservative intellectuals began taking after such programs in the late 1970s.[13] After burning his fingers on national health care in 1994, Clinton spent the rest of the presidency backing away from the very idea of major reform. Henceforth, micro-reform, the more minuscule the better, was all the system could afford. If what was wrong with America could always be cured by what was right with America, then a president's job was merely to fine-tune an already well-functioning polity and render it even "more perfect." Besides, who needed reform when the rising tide of the New Economy was lifting all boats? Entranced by the high-tech sector's seeming ability to turn lead into gold, Clinton hitched his fortunes to Wall Street, Silicon Valley, and Hollywood "content providers" more closely than ever.

GRIDLOCK AND DECAY DID NOT affect all three branches equally either. Initially, the judiciary gained at the other's expense. Given the lassitude of both the Eisenhower White House and a Congress still dominated by Southern Democrats, the Supreme Court was the only ruling institution in Washington capable of undertaking long-overdue structural reforms, hence the only institution capable of enunciating a remotely progressive philosophy of government. An entire generation of liberals came of age believing that the federal judiciary would somehow save America from itself. Yet by the 1960s, a perceptual shift was underway. Congress was as somnolent as ever, but the executive branch was beginning to stir. Kennedy was able to make little headway against the logjam on Capitol Hill, but Johnson scored a key victory by shepherding an epochal Civil Rights Act through Congress in 1965. But when he fell victim to a combination of urban revolt, campus radicalism, and the Vietnamese revolution, it was left to his successor to create the colossus that the world now knows as the US presidency.

It is difficult to write about Richard M. Nixon in a sober, balanced manner given the awesome passions his memory still arouses. For postwar liberals, he was the devil incarnate, a pioneering redbaiter who used every dirty trick in the book to fight his way to the top. Even Eisenhower viewed his vice president with ill-concealed disdain. (When asked at a news conference in August 1960 to cite a major idea that Nixon had contributed to his administration, Ike replied: "If you give me a week, I might think of one."[14]) Compared with JFK and LBJ, however, his policies do not stand out as notably egregious. He spent his presidency trying to fight his way out of the mess that his two predecessors had created in Vietnam, and his treatment of Allende in Chile was fully of a piece with Johnson's treatment of Juan Bosch in the Dominican Republic and Kennedy's treatment of Castro and Diem.

Nixon's creation of the imperial presidency was an example of how, rather than moderating power, the competition generated by American-style checks and balances excites it to new levels of irresponsibility and abuse. Hemmed in by a Democratic Congress on one side and a liberal Supreme Court on the other, Nixon might very well have raised the white flag following his narrow victory in 1968. Instead, he struck out boldly. He escalated the war in Southeast Asia, invading Cambodia and Laos and bombing North Vietnam, while simultaneously moving to isolate Hanoi from its allies in Moscow and Beijing. Faced with an international capitalist economy that had turned seriously rocky, he ended the convertibility of the US dollar to gold and imposed an across-the-board wage-and-price freeze. Such policies were far from uniformly successful. The US economy limped along for the rest of the decade, while the peace treaty that Henry Kissinger negotiated with his North Vietnamese counterpart Le Duc Tho did little to disguise the magnitude of the US defeat. In other ways, though, Nixon's success was stunning. Sensing that international politics had reached a turning point, he succeeded in crystallizing it along new international lines by neutralizing China, promoting *détente* with the Soviet Union, and, in general, preparing the way for the great anti-Communist rollback of 1989–91. Where Moscow and Beijing had formerly vied with one another to see who could be more anti-American, they now competed for US favors.

The United States needed an Oval Office commensurate with its new international role. Congress could wheel and deal, the judiciary could pontificate, but only the White House was capable of both the petty skullduggery and grand international orchestration that Nixon's ambitious program seemed to demand. Arguably, Nixon was merely circling back to the ideas of Woodrow Wilson, who had been campaigning for a reinvigorated presidency ever since his under-graduate days at Princeton. Yet the fantastic increase in American power made for a White House expansion far beyond anything Wilson could have imagined. The president now personified US imperial power, a relationship that the hapless Jimmy Carter helped negatively confirm when his efforts to downsize the Oval Office coincided with a series of devastating foreign policy reversals. What wearing a cardigan sweater on TV and nattering on about "malaise" had to do with inflation, OPEC oil embargoes, or the takeover of the US Embassy in Iran was anybody's guess. But because Carter had failed to live up to the grandeur of the office, it appeared that American power was on the wane. America needed a president who was not afraid to behave in an imperial manner, a role that Ronald Reagan was happy to fill.

In some ways, an American president is still weaker than a Canadian or European prime minister. While pretending to set legislative priorities, he merely goes through the motions knowing that the legislative branch will follow its own lead regardless. He may be head of state, yet Congress's mission is to remind him continually that he is not the head of government, an office that in America does not really exist.* In other respects, however, a US president is a good deal more powerful. Surrounded by courtiers, intelligence agencies, and military units at his beck and call, he is free to launch invasions or order covert operations any time, day or night, without fear of contradiction from his cabinet or any of his subordinates. Indeed, he is

---

* With its multiple power centers, the United States lacks a government as other nations understand the term. While phrases like "the government announced today" or "the government declared tonight" are common in the British press, an American reader would be puzzled were he to come across any such combination in the US. Who or what, he would want to know, might this "government" be? Is it the White House, the Pentagon, the Speaker of the House, or what? This is why the *New York Times* and all newspapers that follow its lead (which means the entire American fourth estate) is careful to attribute specific acts to specific ruling institutions. Thus, it is "the White House announced today" or "the State Department declared tonight." Instead of "government," Americans follow eighteenth-century British usage in referring to each presidency as an "administration."

expected to engage in such unilateral displays, which is why Reagan's 1983 invasion of Grenada, George Bush's 1989 invasion of Panama, or Bill Clinton's frequent use of cruise missiles met with bipartisan approval. Short of total warfare, a US president has *carte blanche* to attack whom he pleases virtually anywhere in the world. The only check on his power is the fear that one of his targets might someday strike back, a fear, needless to say, that no imperial power can afford to admit.

The 1998 Republican impeachment drive has been termed an effort to cut the presidency down to proper republican size.[15] Yet the GOP targeted Clinton not because his behavior was too imperial, but because it was not imperial enough. He was a draft-dodging, pot-smoking child of the '60s who was unable to control his libido and was therefore judged to have demeaned the office. Rather than reducing the Oval Office, the GOP offensive was an attempt to blow it up to ever more gargantuan size.

THUS WAS THE SCENE SET for the year 2000 elections. Never had the mystique of the presidency been more overblown or the election process longer and more expensive. Anxious to establish their middle-of-the-road credentials, the two leading candidates spoke in airy generalities, proclaimed their love of the people at every opportunity, and utilized the most advanced sales techniques in hope of increasing market share. They convened focus groups, conducted surveys, analyzed voter profiles, and test-marketed slogans and proposals. Yet not only did the two sides' super-sophisticated marketing techniques wind up canceling each other out, they ended up turning voters off. Faced with the political equivalent of Coke and Pepsi, voters responded like jaded consumers faced with two rival brands. Basing their decision on increasingly trivial criteria having to do with appearance or personal demeanor, they ended up splitting nearly down the middle. It was not as if Americans had nothing to discuss. Thanks to capital punishment, wage stagnation, global warming, the gun culture, and a punitive yet pointless War on Drugs, they had a great deal. Yet Gore, for one, was either too cautious or compromised to take any of those issues on. The economic gap between working- and upper-class Americans had widened during his eight years as vice president, the War on Drugs had intensified, while half-hearted efforts at gun control had come to naught. Rather than reducing consumption of fossil fuels, the chief culprit in global warming, the administration had allowed it to accelerate. As a supporter of the death penalty, Gore was hardly in a position to criticize his opponent for presiding over more than a hundred executions during his years in the Texas governor's mansion. Indeed, the most he could do was to complain that Bush had failed to install certain legal safeguards designed to make sure that the wrong person was not executed.[16] Capital punishment was fine as long as it was administered fairly. In the end, the only issue that Gore felt comfortable discussing was the rising cost of prescription drugs, which he made the centerpiece of his campaign.

The system served to constrict political debate when it most needed to expand. When Ralph Nader persisted in his quixotic third-party campaign, liberals turned on him in a fury. He was a spoiler, they said. By attacking Gore from the left, he was playing into the hands of the right. Although voters in other countries could select from a half-dozen parties or more, Nader was wrong to argue that Americans had a right to select from more than just two. Although they had been choosing either Republicans or Democrats in virtually all elections since 1856, this limited menu was all the system could afford. Judging from the level of Democratic anger at Nader after election day—former presidential candidate Michael Dukakis threatened to "strangle the guy with my bare hands if he helps George W. Bush beat Al Gore"—anyone who said otherwise was guilty of criminal irresponsibility.[17]

BUSH CUT AN ESPECIALLY pathetic figure on the campaign trail. Inarticulate and ill at ease, he was unable to present voters with anything by way of an alternative vision or a comprehensive critique of where the Democrats had gone wrong. His malapropisms were legendary. Referring to Clinton's verbal contortions during the Monica Lewinsky affair, he declared at one point, "Never again in the halls of Washington, DC, do I want to have to make explanations I can't explain."[18] Attacking the Democrats for opposing Social Security privatization, he shouted at another campaign rally, "They want the federal government controlling the Social Security, like it's some kind of federal program."[19] Nonetheless, he was not without certain strengths. As both general manager of the Texas Rangers baseball team and governor, he had raised affability to an art form, a skill that now enabled him to disguise his hard-right views and persuade at least some voters that he was really a moderate in conservative clothing. (In fact, he was a hard rightist in moderate clothing.) He practiced a treacly kind of rhetoric that some found disarming. He also enjoyed the backing of an unusually united and powerful business class. Thanks to a hyper-Jeffersonian state constitution dating from the waning days of Reconstruction, political power in Texas was even more fragmented than in the country as a whole. Not only was the governor's office weak, but the legislature was weak also, with real power residing with some two hundred semiautonomous administrative boards governing everything from funeral parlors to prisons.[20] Fragmentation of this sort has the same effect at the state level as it does at the federal: it eliminates effective public oversight, marginalizes democracy, while insuring that the real business of government takes place behind closed doors where wealthy businessmen rub shoulders with their cronies in government. According to one study, Texas has seen a succession of "superrich ... conservatives and reactionaries" thrust themselves into state politics and win one battle after another with the "largely depoliticized masses." According to another study:

> [T]he governor is commonly a member of the business elite and builds direct, intimate relationships with powerful local, state, and national elites. ... [T]he governor's power, position, and authority lie in intricate patterns of formal and informal authority ... adequate enough to serve successfully the conservative goals of small government, low taxes, and low spending.[21]

A splintered governing structure thus allowed an unusually unified ruling class to gather up the reins behind the scenes. Dominated by oilmen opposed to any and all government programs except those benefiting their own industry, Texas businessmen were grateful to Bush for his unstinting efforts on their behalf and anxious to return the favor. When the crunch came, they flooded his campaign with money, moral support, and expertise.

The great crack-up that began on election day was the product of constitutional machinery so long overdue for an overhaul that the people who had come to depend on it had forgotten what the very word meant. In essence, the problem lay with a two-century-old section in Article II describing how members of the Electoral College are to be chosen. "Each State," it declares, "shall appoint, in such Manner as the Legislature thereof may direct, a Number of Electors, equal to the whole Number of Senators and Representatives to which the State may be entitled in the Congress." Just as Article I gave the states wide latitude in electing members of Congress, Article II gave them equal elbowroom in electing presidents. Even though the states would eventually allow at least some portion of the electorate to choose the electors themselves via a popular vote, Article II was a reminder that they did so voluntarily, without conceding anything to the federal government. Although the 1965 Civil Rights Act would eventually allow Washington to intervene in local elections in order to prevent the most egregious forms of racial discrimination, the general assumption was that intervention would be the exception rather than the rule and that control would essentially continue with the states.

Whatever sense state autonomy of this sort might have made in the 1780s, it made no sense in the year 2000. In the modern era, any government seeing itself as democratic necessarily sees the conduct of free and fair national elections as its highest responsibility. It sees them in this way not only for the people's sake but so that it can establish its own democratic credentials at home and abroad. Yet rather than placing responsibility squarely in the hands of the national government, America's superannuated Constitution placed it in the hands of states whose relationship to the federal government it viewed as fundamentally antagonistic.

This is why events spun so quickly out of control after November 7. Florida was not the only state where voters had trouble. Mistakes, technical glitches, and organizational foul-ups snarled voting in Albuquerque, New Mexico, where some 60,000 absentee ballots initially went uncounted; in Scott County, Iowa, where Bush wound up with 2,000 extra votes due to a blurry fax; in Outagamie County, Wisconsin, where a typo gave him hundreds more, and in Portland, Oregon, where unidentified people posing as poll workers in the street made off with an unknown number of absentee ballots. In Selma, Alabama, white election officials conspired to hold down black voting through such time-honored stratagems as limiting voting hours, putting polling places beyond the reach of public transportation, and assigning voters to different precincts for municipal, state, and federal elections, a tactic designed to discourage and confuse.[22] But steps like these are exactly what one would expect in a system that places nearly total control in a swarm of local officials of varying degrees of competence and good faith.

Odds were that glitches like these would threaten the outcome in at least one state, and the Sunshine State turned out to be it. Yet not only did the Constitution give Florida ample leeway in running the election, it gave the state's Republican establishment ample leeway in deciding whether an obviously flawed tally should be allowed to stand. When Gore called for a statewide recount, the Bush campaign rejected the idea as unwarranted and impractical. When he called for a recount in just four counties out of sixty-seven, the Republicans said it would be unfair to count some and not all. Desperate to prevent the Democrats from erasing Bush's lead, the Republican strategy was to file nuisance lawsuits, move for changes of venue, and then complain that the recount was taking too much time. When a dispute over a group of absentee ballots ended up before a black woman judge whom Republican lawyers feared was dangerously liberal, they tried five different ways to prevent her from ruling. They called on her to recuse herself, asked an appeals court to dismiss her, filed another appeal when that didn't work, tried to have the case consolidated with a case before another judge, and finally asked for a jury trial.[23] (Ironically, the judge ultimately decided in the GOP's favor.) When the Florida Supreme Court blocked Secretary of State Katherine Harris, co-chairman of Bush's Florida campaign, from declaring her candidate the winner, the Republican-controlled state legislature vowed to award him the election itself.

It was an astonishing display of raw political muscle. When a screaming mob of Republican activists intimidated the Miami election board into aborting a recount that might have put Gore over the top, Democrats fired off another round of lawsuits. But it was to no avail. A conservative state judge in Tallahassee turned them down, the state supreme court ordered the count to resume but then failed to allocate enough time, while a brazenly partisan US Supreme Court decided that a state government had a constitutional right to hijack a national election after all.

"The individual citizen," the Supreme Court's conservative majority declared, "has no federal constitutional right to vote for electors for the president of the United States unless and until the state legislature chooses a statewide election as the means to implement its power to appoint members of the Electoral College." State officials, in other words, were not required to hold free, honest, and fair presidential elections; in fact, they were not required to hold presidential elections at all. Not only does the pre-modern US Constitution deny the federal government the power to establish its own democratic credential, it allows the states to undermine them at will.

THE IMAGE OF A MOB of angry Republicans pounding on doors and windows, roughing up Democrats, and shouting, "Stop the count! Stop the fraud!" will be as long associated with the events of November–December 2000 as Barbara Jordan's impassioned remarks were with Watergate. While America had certainly seen its share of tumultuous demonstrations, this was the first time in memory that one of the two major parties had used mob violence to cut short a vote count. Although Republicans insisted that the protesters were merely concerned citizens, the crowd included a number of high-level GOP operatives: a policy analyst in the office of House Majority Whip Tom Delay, an attorney on the staff of the House Judiciary Committee, a staffer with the National Republican Congressional Committee, a former aide to Senator Fred D. Thompson, and so on.[24] Rather than rank-and-file citizens, these were dedicated frontline soldiers. The fracas they staged worked because it came at a moment of acute vulnerability when no one was capable of stepping in and bringing order out of chaos. Amid such a vacuum, the Republicans were able to step in and deliver a devastating blow. Instead of disowning such tactics, both Bush and vice presidential candidate Dick Cheney congratulated the organizers and joked about the assault via telephone at a Republican victory bash a few nights later in Fort Lauderdale.[25]

The *Wall Street Journal* editorial page, the semi-official bulletin board of the US far right, was especially provocative during this period. Quick to accuse Gore of launching a coup attempt merely because he was seeking an honest recount, it featured articles by such rightwing spokesmen as former drug czar William Bennett accusing Gore of an "illegitimate" bid for power and "a massive campaign to subvert the outcome." *Wall Street Journal* columnist Paul A. Gigot crowed that the GOP's Miami assault was a neatly timed "bourgeois riot ... [that] could end up saving the presidency for George W. Bush."[26]

But it was left to an obscure professor at the Naval War College named Mackubin Thomas Owens to show what was ultimately at stake. Furious that Gore campaign workers in Florida had challenged a batch of absentee ballots from overseas military personnel, Owens fired off a guest editorial in the *Journal* on November 22, the day of the Miami riot, accusing Democrats of "engag[ing] in an unprece-dented campaign against the military ... in the name of multiculturalism, feminism, and the politics of 'sexual orientation.'" "What is at stake in this culture war," he wrote, "is nothing less than the future effectiveness of the military as an institution." Because "the military places a premium on unit cohesion and morale," it emphasizes "such martial virtues as courage, both physical and moral, a sense of honor and duty, discipline, a professional code of conduct, and loyalty." These were qualities "foreign to most civilians," particularly the gay, feminist, and multicultural civilians that he said the Democratic Party largely represents.[27]

Could anything have been clearer? Republican putschists in Miami stood for the Constitution and the military, according to Owens and his editors, while the Democrats were attempting to undermine America's defenses in the name of feminism, homosexuality, and racial diversity. In just over two weeks, the constitutional crisis had laid bare the deepest divisions in US society. Instead of Republicans and Democrats, the conflict was now between stern warriors and decadent bohemians. As much as Democrats wanted Gore to win, they were taken back by the ferocity of the Republican offensive. What would the GOP do if Gore succeeded in overturning the results in court? Would more "bourgeois riots" ensue? Would military officers rise in revolt? Such *Seven Days in May* scenarios no longer seemed so outlandish.

From that point on, the courts increasingly deferred to the Republican *fait accompli*. On December 9, conservative Supreme Court Justice Antonin Scalia ordered a halt to the recount on the grounds that it threatened "irreparable harm to petitioner, and to the country, by casting a cloud upon what he claims to be the legitimacy of his election"—as if cutting the recount short would not undermine democratic legitimacy as well. Three days later, Scalia joined with the court's four other conservative members in terminating the recount altogether on the grounds that the clock had run out. Gore supporters were aghast. In an eloquent dissent, liberal Justice John Paul Stevens wrote that the decision "can only lend credence to the most cynical appraisal" of the judiciary's role. "Although we may never know with certainty the identity of the winner of this year's presidential election," he said, "the identity of the loser is clear. It is the nation's confidence in the judge as an impartial guardian of the rule of law."

But if the nation's confidence as a whole was shaken, at least one individual's was not. Shortly after the ruling, Laurence H. Tribe, the dean of liberal constitutionalists, who had argued before the court in Gore's behalf, called on his client to fall on his sword. "I think the gracious thing is to accept even if one disagrees with the decision of the Supreme Court," the Harvard law professor declared. "I think that Vice President Gore has the kind of reverence for the Supreme Court as an institution that he will really not undertake to be less than complete and gracious in his acceptance of the result."[28] Reverence for the high court required the subordination of the popular will to that of the judicial priesthood. After taking a day to consider his options, Gore did as instructed. "Over the library of one of our great law schools," he noted in a televised address, "is inscribed the motto: 'Not under man, but under God and law.' That's the ruling principle of American freedom, the source of our democratic liberties. I've tried to make it my guide throughout this contest, as it has guided America's deliberations of all the complex issues of the past five weeks." The bottom line was that he had no choice but to accede to the Supreme Court's decision and end his campaign.[29]

Although the press universally applauded the speech, no one as usual paused to consider precisely what Gore was saying about the nature of American democracy. "Not under man, but under God and law," which appears over the Harvard Law School library, was the motto of Henry de Bracton, author of *De legibus et consuetudinibus Angliae* ("On the Laws and Customs of England"), who served as chief royal judge in the mid-thirteenth century under Henry III. The principle it advanced has nothing to do with modern democracy— which, needless to say, was still centuries off—and everything to do with the medieval concept of law as a pre-existing entity that was not of society but over it. Rather than a utilitarian instrument for the people to use in the here-and-now, the first principle of popular sovereignty, it represented a concept of the law as something for people to worship and adore, to struggle to understand, but most of all to obey. Although medieval political theory viewed law as something that a particular people might possess, as one authority has noted, it did not imply

> that law was the creature of a people, dependent upon their will, and capable of being changed by their volition. The order of ideas was rather reversed: the folk as a communal body was perhaps more truly conceived to be made by their law, much as a living body might be identified with its principle of organization.[30]

What Gore was advancing was thus a pre-modern concept of constitutionalism, one in which the law makes the people rather than the people making the law. What he was saying, in essence, was that although the voters had decided one way, the law had decided another, and the latter verdict, according to Gore, was the only one that mattered. Instead of basing democracy on popular sovereignty, he was basing it on the opposite: the people's concession of power to an immutable legal structure beyond their command.

The election demonstrated that the party that controlled the constitutional apparatus was the one that controlled political power. The historical analogy that comes most immediately to mind is the "aristocratic reaction" in eighteenth-century France when the nobility began making increasing use of its ancient constitutional prerogatives to hold down a rising middle class. As a conservative body, the aristocracy's goal was to take advantage of an increasingly sclerotic system to see to it that money and power flowed only to those who could prove they were of noble birth. It had tradition and privilege on its side, while the middle class had nothing but talent and numbers, qualities that that the *ancien régime* failed to recognize as valid.[31] As the more conservative of the two bourgeois parties, the Republicans enjoyed a similar advantage in the year 2000 in an increasingly conservative system that elevates states' rights, separation of powers, and the like over simple majority rule. The more it championed such privileges, the greater its hostility to elementary democratic norms grew. As a top Republican lobbyist crowed while strolling alongside Jeb Bush following a triumphant session of the Florida state legislature: "I got everything. I don't know what the poor people got, but the rich people are happy and I'm ready to go home."[32] This was the happy cry of a class warrior increasingly adept at manipulating the political structure to the benefit of an increasingly narrow stratum at the top.

PREDICTABLY, THE YEAR 2000 ELECTION mess led to calls to repeal the Electoral College. One came from Hillary Clinton, who declared a few days after her election victory in New York: "I have always thought we had outlived the need for an Electoral College, and now that I am going to the Senate, I am going to try to do what I can to make clear that the popular vote, the will of the people, should be followed."[33] Another came from New York University law professor Ronald Dworkin, who wrote in the *New York Review of Books*:

We now have the best chance ever to junk [this] anachronistic and dangerous eighteenth-century system. The public should demand that Congress begin a process of constitutional amendment that would eliminate that system, root and branch, and substitute for it the direct election of the president and vice president by a plurality of the national popular vote.[34]

Yet a bit of simple arithmetic shows why any such constitutional amendment is out of the question. Not only does the Electoral College triple the political clout of voters in the seven least populous states that elect just one member of the House, it doubles the clout of those in six other states that elect two members of the House and augments by roughly two-thirds the clout of those in four others that elect just three. This is a good deal more than the bare minimum of just thirteen states that the two-thirds/three-fourths rule in Article V allows to veto any and all efforts at constitutional reform. Barring some miraculous change of heart, consequently, small states that are overwhelmingly rural and white can be counted on to block any change that would place their citizens on an equal footing with those in large states that are urban and multiracial. Although the Supreme Court has repeatedly declared since *Baker v. Carr* in 1962 that one person-one vote must prevail at the state and local level, the Constitution effectively bars it at the federal. Just as "we the people" were powerless to do anything about slavery prior to the Civil War, "we the people" are now powerless to do away with an arrangement as patently unfair as the Electoral College. Rather than guaranteeing democratic liberties, the Ancient Constitution denies them.

The dimensions of the Republican victory only gradually became apparent in the weeks following the Supreme Court's decision in *Bush v. Gore*. For the first time in postwar history, the GOP had made a clean sweep, gaining control not just of the executive and legislative branches, but of the judiciary, too. Chief Justice William Rehnquist, seventy-six years old at the time of the December 12 ruling, could retire secure in the knowledge that his successor would be someone he would find ideologically congenial. While hardly the first conservative to occupy the Oval Office, George W. Bush was the first Southern conservative since before the Civil War, an important distinction in terms of America's highly charged geopolitics. Meanwhile, Al Gore left Washington to teach journalism, Bill Clinton huddled in disgrace in suburban New York amid a growing furor over a series of his last-minute presidential pardons, while Hillary Clinton, widely considered a possible presidential contender in 2004 or 2008, was similarly neutralized. As the liberal economist Robert Kuttner put it in a magazine column the following January: "It's like a country after a bloodless coup d'état. Daily life goes on. The tame media makes soothing noises. Rituals of democracy endure. The out-party simulates opposition, toothlessly."[35] Yet the substance of democracy had been lost.

6

IS THERE A WAY OUT?

IT IS AUGUST 2004. After nearly four years of hard-right policies under George W. Bush, Democrats are thirsting for revenge. They want nothing more than a rematch with the Republican team that they believe stole the 2000 presidential election. Accordingly, the party once again makes Al Gore the standard-bearer. Looking trim and only a little grayer, the former vice president bounds onto the stage at the Democratic National Convention as his wife Tipper is winding up her remarks. Jubilantly, he gives her another of those long smackers that have become a personal trademark. Then he launches into his speech.

Coolly, he runs through the Bush administration's record over the previous four years, its tax cuts for the rich, its budget cuts for everyone else, and its scuttling of the Kyoto Accords on global warming. His manner is passionate, yet controlled. Instead of moving forward, he says, Americans have had to stand by while Republicans turned back the clock. Instead of seeing their country advance, they have seen it regress to the days of Ronald Reagan and the elder George Bush. This is all quite galling. But what is even more galling, Gore continues, is that these are not the policies that Americans voted for. A clear majority who voted in 2000 for either the Democrats or the Greens voted in favor of environmental protection, stepped-up spending for healthcare and the poor, and a woman's right to choose. Yet even though the Democrats alone won by more than half a million votes, they wound up with a Republican who has waged war on all three.

The candidate pauses. Ten or fifteen seconds tick by as the delegates think back to the events of four years earlier—the butterfly ballots, the goon squads, the police roadblocks scaring away black voters. "With all due respect to my opponent," Gore resumes finally, "this must never happen again. Never again must the will of the people be flouted. Never again must votes be ignored. Never again should the outcome in a single state be allowed to offset the popular vote nationwide. As great as our Founding Fathers were, they were uncertain as to whether they wanted America to be a democracy or an indirectly elected republic. For a long time, Americans themselves were not sure either. But now, after more than two centuries, we have made up our minds. We want a democracy. We want a democracy based on the will of the people. We want a democracy that counts every vote. We want a democracy dedicated to the proposition that all Americans, male or female, black or white, rich or poor, are created equal." Then peering out across a sea of white, black, and brown faces: "We want a democracy that does not give some states greater clout in presidential elections and other states—big states that are multiracial and urban—less clout merely because something called the Electoral College says that's the way it ought to be. Democracy means one person-one vote regardless of the color of your skin, your gender or sexual orientation, or whether you live in California or Wyoming."

This is the red meat the audience has been waiting for. After a full minute of wild cheering, the nominee holds up his hand for silence. "Now, as we all know, it is effectively impossible to change the Electoral College by amending the Constitution. Some seven hundred proposed amendments have been in introduced in Congress over the last two centuries in an effort to reform or abolish this system.[1] That's a little more than one every four months. Yet all have failed. Hillary Clinton, our esteemed senator from New York, was the latest to try, and she has failed also. Over the years, the states that benefit disproportionately from the Electoral College have made it plain that they will never consent to the slightest alteration in the status quo, and unfortunately there are too many small states that feel that way to ever allow such an amendment to pass. Therefore, the Electoral College is destined to remain on the books for as long as anyone can foresee.

"But that's not the end of the story," Gore continues. "Even if we can't change the Constitution, there is a way that we can render the Electoral College a dead letter. All we have to do is enter into a simple agreement. I propose that my opponent and I both make a pledge. Regardless of the outcome in the Electoral College, I propose that we both promise to abide by the popular vote and only by the popular vote. As soon as the vote totals are known, I propose that the loser issue a statement conceding defeat and releasing his electors to vote for the other side. While the electors will not have to switch their vote, I am sure that most will follow their candidate's advice and obey the democratic will. Assuming that is the case, a very important precedent will have been set. The Electoral College will continue to meet every four years. But henceforth it will become nothing more than a formality, a body whose purpose is to ratify the results of a free election and acknowledge that the people have spoken. Without changing so much as a comma in the Constitution, we can insure that power will once again reside with the people, from whom it should never have left. America is a democracy, and in a democracy 'we the people' rule."

More cheering erupts.

"I hereby take that pledge. I challenge my opponent to do the same ...."

IN AN ESSAY PUBLISHED a few years ago, a University of Texas law professor named Sanford Levinson posed an intriguing question: Is a constitutional amendment adopted in accordance with the provisions in Article V really an amendment?[2] This may sound like a typical academic jawbreaker, yet it is in fact highly relevant in terms of the current American predicament. In one sense, of course, an amendment approved by two-thirds of each house plus three-fourths of the states does represent change in that it tacks on additional words that modify to some degree the preceding text. When Congress and the states approved an amendment prohibiting "the manufacture, sale, or transportation of intoxicating liquors" shortly after World War I, the result was not only to ban alcoholic beverages, but to alter the structure of federal–state relations. Where previously the Constitution had allowed Congress to regulate interstate commerce only, the Eighteenth Amendment allowed it to extend its reach so as to cover at least one aspect of intrastate commerce as well. Ironically, a neo-Jeffersonian campaign wound up contributing to the growth of big government, the Jeffersonian *bête noire*.

In another sense, though, the amendment changed nothing. Indeed, by virtue of its ratification in accordance with the complicated provisions set forth in Article V, the Eighteenth Amendment confirmed that rules dating from the late eighteenth century were as binding as ever. Rather than a departure from past practice,

Prohibition therefore represented a continuation. It was an admission, in effect, that the Founders were still paramount and that their rules still prevailed. The amendment served a dual purpose—to ban alcohol and to confirm that Americans must submit to pre-existing constitutional principles—which is one reason why the political atmosphere in 1920s America was so stiflingly conservative.

Change that takes place in accordance with Article V is licensed change, whereas real change means a departure from any such arrangement. The beauty of the foregoing Al Gore scenario is that it entails a genuine rejection of Madisonian dictates. Not only would its goal be to render inoperative an important governing institution, one central to the Founders' concept of checks and balances and separation of powers, but it would introduce an entirely new principle, the notion that the people have a right to reshape political institutions not in their capacity as citizens of the separate states, but as citizens of a single nation. "Electoral despotism" of this sort would have Jefferson spinning in his grave, but that is precisely the point. It would be the first step toward knocking the Founders off their pedestal and hence a step toward the Constitution's de-sanctification. Rather than a sacred mystery, the goal is to enable Americans to see their governing institutions as something created not by a race of giants, but by a group of decidedly flawed individuals.

If Al Gore were to take such a step, what would be the consequence? For starters, we can assume that there would be no shortage of eminent constitutional authorities telling him that such a step would be illegal. If the Constitution says that only the Electoral College can choose a president, then that's what the Constitution says. Yet the experts would be wrong. The law cannot prevent a candidate from voluntarily withdrawing from the race, nor can it prevent individual electors from changing their votes once he has given them permission to change sides. If Gore stuck to his guns, such protests would soon die away.

We can also assume that the legal professoriat would not be the only ones to react adversely, but that George W. Bush would, too. He would undoubtedly reject any such offer out of hand, not because it would mean surrendering a crucial political advantage, needless to say, but because he believes in God, the Constitution, and standing by the laws that made America great. Dubya's response would be all too predictable: "The Electoral College is how the Founding Fathers wanted us to choose the president, and I would no more disobey the Founding Fathers than I would disobey the word of God." The secret joy that would surge through Republican hearts would be all too predictable also. What more could the GOP ask for than a Democrat campaigning against the Constitution? Chortling that Gore had handed them his head on a silver platter, they would immediately fan out across the country, confident that the people would no more vote against the Founders than the flag.

But if Gore stuck to his guns in this regard also, the results could be dramatic. In essence, it would mean transforming the presidential election into a constitutional referendum. Instead of merely Bush versus Gore, the question before voters would now be that of the Electoral College versus the popular vote. Instead of concentrating on a handful of swing states as they did in 2000, the logic of the Democrats' position would compel them to concentrate on the big urban states where their strength is concentrated. Formerly, it had not mattered whether turnout in such states was fifty, sixty, or seventy percent as long as they remained firmly in the Democratic camp. Once the outcome was secure, each additional vote was superfluous, which is why campaign workers saved their energy for those states where the electoral votes were still up for grabs. But now that the

Democrats had pledged to disregard the Electoral College, such considerations would no longer apply. With every last vote suddenly mattering a great deal, Democratic campaign workers in California, New York, and so on would have an incentive to ring every doorbell, canvass every ghetto street, and scour every union hall and homeless shelter in search of Gore supporters who had not yet made it to the polls.

By pledging to abide by the popular vote, Gore would transform how the election was argued and fought. In mobilizing the people against the Electoral College, he would be mobilizing them against a system that favors small over large states, whites over blacks and Hispanics, and farmers and ranchers over subway riders and commuters in crowded urban and suburban districts. Whether he liked it or not, he would be stirring up class passions against a ticket headed by a pair of Texas oilmen and backed by some eighty-six percent of major corporate CEOs.[3] Instead of a struggle for control of the White House, the race would now be a struggle for control of the political system itself, a struggle framed from the start by the issues of race and class.

Given the immense demographic disparities among the fifty states—ten states as of the year 2000 account for fifty-four percent of the US population, while ten others account for under three percent[4]—such a contest would render more likely rather than less the sort of split decision in which one candidate wins the popular vote and the other wins the electoral. This is what happened in 2000, yet in one respect the results a second time around would be very different. Rather than surprised by the outcome, voters on both sides would be prepared. All eyes would be on Bush to see what he did. Would he try to take the White House despite once again losing the popular vote? After specifically voting against the Electoral College, would the majority let him? Depending on his response, the situation could be nothing less than revolutionary. Even if by some fluke, moreover, Bush won both the popular and electoral vote, the cat would still be out of the bag. Eventually, the question would be sure to come up again, and when it did, the outcome would likely be very different. The days in which the US Constitution could carry on in blithe defiance of modern democratic norms would be numbered.

OF COURSE, THERE IS A GOOD DEAL that makes this scenario implausible as well. As we have seen, such a step would be a radical departure in terms of America's hidebound politics, and someone given to quoting a thirteenth-century legal authority like Henry de Bracton is not generally one for radical departures. Indeed, everything that Al Gore had learned in the course of his long political career would tell him not to embark on such a wild and risky course. Every adviser, every pundit, every academic hoping for a White House job would tell him that the safest thing would be to mount a campaign very much like the one he mounted in 2000 in the hope of gaining the extra sliver of voters needed to put him over the top. Rather than paying less attention to swing states, they would counsel him to pay more. Instead of attacking the Electoral College, they would advise that he wrap himself up in the Constitution all the more completely. All indications are that Gore would do as he was told, just as he did in December 2000. Rather than stirring the people up, he would lull them back to sleep.

Moreover, the real danger from a Democratic point of view is not that a radical departure of this sort would fizzle, but that it would succeed all too well, igniting passions that they would prefer to remain dormant. Although leftists such as the late Michael Harrington argued that the Democrats were a working-class party along the lines of Labour in Britain or the European social democrats, nothing could be farther from the truth. Rather than heightening or even acknowledging class differences, the Democratic Party exists to obscure them under a thick layer of patriotism, nostalgia, and American exceptionalism. While a politician like Al Gore is not above stirring up low-grade populist resentment against some of the GOP's more egregious abuses, a totalizing concept like class is alien to his makeup. Rather than encouraging conflict between labor and capital, Gore, a former senator from a right-to-work state, would do everything in his power to discourage it. Comity, not conflict, is his patriotic ideal.

Challenging the Constitution even obliquely is also alien to his makeup. In calling on voters to render the Electoral College a dead letter, Gore could not avoid encouraging them to grapple with some of the Constitution's other less palatable features. A Senate organized on the principle of equal state representation regardless of population—shouldn't the people figure out some way of sidelining this pre-modern relic as well? Shouldn't they see to it that the Supreme Court never hands down a judicial atrocity like the one in December 2000? Aren't federal–state relations also due for an overhaul?

The answer is that they are. Indeed, it is hard to imagine an aspect of America's Ancient Constitution that is not in need of being rethought. Yet as someone steeped from childhood in America's superannuated eighteenth-century politics, Gore would likely see democratic change of this sort essentially the same way that the Founders would have seen it, i.e. as something irrational and anarchic. Since he can't imagine an alternative to the *ancien régime*, any attempt to replace it would strike him as purely destructive. His only choice is to somehow make the existing system work. As far as he would be concerned, there is simply no alternative to the House, Senate, and presidency revolving around an immovable Constitution, just as there is no alternative to the sun and planets continuing to revolve around an immovable earth—or is it the other way around?

On the other hand, stranger things have happened. Respectable politicians who open the door to structural reform and then get more than they bargained for are not unknown. Neither are ultra-establishmentarians who none the less recognize that society has reached a dead end and that radical change is unavoidable. Al Gore could usher in democracy, or democracy could usher itself in without him. Regardless of what happens, the United States cannot avoid the problem of what to do with an ossified, eighteenth-century Constitution forever.

Of course, this is just one way by which US society might begin the process of jettisoning the past and advancing to a higher stage of political development. While a revolt against the Electoral College would be one possibility, a revolt against the Senate would be another, while a revolt against the Second Amendment (about which, more below) would be a third. All would be potentially revolutionary because all would entail a single, unified people extending their sway over the governing system as a whole. Each would mean the creation of a force, i.e. popular sovereignty, that the Constitution does not recognize and, in fact, is designed to prevent. Yet it is precisely the need to do the forbidden in this way that propels society forward.

What is to be done? Any program of democratic constitutional reform in the United States would likely involve some or all of the following elements:

Proportional representation: A feature of all modern parliamentary systems except the British, Canadian, and Australian, this is best understood as an attempt to give new meaning to the principle of one person-one vote. Although details differ, PR essentially entails voting from a common ballot throughout the country. Once voters have chosen from a list of competing parties, slates, or coalitions, representation in the national assembly is allocated according to each party's share of the national tally. In a hundred-seat assembly, the party that gets twenty-five percent of the vote gets twenty-five seats, the party that gets fifteen percent gets fifteen seats, and so on. No one's vote is wasted because he is a liberal in a conservative congressional district or a conservative in a liberal district. Because voters have a dozen or more parties to choose from, no one's vote is debased by virtue of being cast for a party whose only virtue is that it is "the lesser of two evils."

As any reader of the *New York Times*, a consistent opponent of PR, can attest, the system is rife with problems. Rather than the Gibraltar-like stability of a two-party system dating from the 1850s (which no longer seems so stable in the wake of the 2000 election debacle), it often encourages a proliferation of small parties that can lead to shifting alliances and frequent changes of government. Rather than decisiveness and bold action, it can lead to Italian-style political paralysis and backroom deal-making in which party leaders trade ministerial portfolios, favors, and whatnot back and forth in order to hammer out what the *Times* usually refers to as yet another "unstable coalition government."

All too true. Yet the same thing can be said about free speech: rather than clarity, it, too, often results in muddle and confusion. When it does, though, the answer is not less freedom but more, which is to say the freedom to stand up and tell the other speakers that they are going about it all wrong, that they need to organize debate along more coherent lines, that they should not interrupt, etc., etc. If the major parties habitually engage in seamy backroom negotiations, similarly, the solution is to organize a party that flushes them out.

Rather than belaboring politics with myriad rules and regulations whose purpose is to protect democracy against itself, the solution is to free up democracy so that it can reorganize itself on a more rational basis.

What liberals see as PR's great failing—its encouragement of small parties—is really its great strength. A mega-party like the Democrats resembles nothing so much as the Church of England, an immense state-supported institution that no one believes in and that people attend solely through force of habit. On the other hand, at least some of the parties that spring up in more democratic systems are not afraid to believe in something. Rather than fuzziness, they strive for clarity. Instead of micro-changes, their aim is to transform the whole of society. Any citizen of a democracy who is denied access to such a party system is denied the full value of his vote.

Unfortunately, it is not enough to defend proportional representation against its enemies—it must also be defended against its friends. In the United States, groups such as the Center for Voting and Democracy in Bethesda, Maryland, have promoted an anodyne version of PR as a harmless add-on that can be safely injected without disturbing the larger structure. As such advocates are fond of pointing out, the fuss and bother of Florida in November–December 2000 could have been avoided if the state's twenty-five electoral votes had been divided on the basis of each candidate's share of the statewide total (which, of course, would have given Gore the election). The problem of wasted votes in congressional elections could be similarly reduced merely by dividing up congressional seats on the basis of each party's share of the statewide total. If sixty percent of Californians vote Democratic, then the Democrats should get sixty percent of California's fifty-two House seats. If ten percent vote Green, then the Greens should get five seats, and so on.

Since Article I declares that "[t]he Times, Places and Manner of holding Elections for Senators and Representatives, shall be prescribed in each State by the Legislature thereof," such an approach would be perfectly constitutional. But at least two objections arise. One is that in a system as ossified as the US, even eminently safe and sensible reforms like these are doomed from the outset. The system is so inured against change that it is unable to tolerate even the most modest. With both Democrats and Republicans desperate to maintain their strongholds, neither would agree to any change that might in any way benefit the other. Instead, each will happily wait for the opposing side to make the first move, which, of course, it never will.

The other objection is that any attempt to inject proportional representation into one branch while remaining silent about far worse abuses in another is a travesty. Democratic reform in the House would be welcome, yet the democratic inadequacies of the House pale in comparison with those of the Senate, perhaps the most unrepresentative legislative body in the world. Equal state representation was bad enough in the late eighteenth century when the ratio between the most populous and the least populous state was a mere eleven to one. But it is far worse now that it is sixty-nine to one and rising. Where a Senate majority could have been cobbled together out of members representing just thirty-three percent of the US population in 1810, by 1970 it could have been cobbled together out of members representing just seventeen.[5] By allowing thirteen states representing as little as five percent of the population to block any constitutional amendment, the Article V amending process is even more unrepresentative, while Article V's final clause precluding any alteration of the principle of equal state representation unless every state agrees is the ultimate affront.

Any system of proportional representation that does not attack misrepresentation on this scale is not worthy of the name. Rather than avoiding the problem of what to do about the Senate on the grounds that it is too intractable or too controversial, the Senate should be the first target at which PR advocates take aim.

Campaign finance: Financial corruption, of course, is a violation of one person-one vote because it allows the wealthy to multiply their political power beyond their actual numbers. Yet campaign finance reform will inevitably prove ineffectual in the United States as long as it remains divorced from the question of constitutional structure. The reason, simply, is that the more complicated the structure, the greater the number of places in which power brokers, influence peddlers, and the like can hide. When legislation must follow a long and tortuous route to passage, then every twist and turn, fork or ford, is an opportunity for some subcommittee chairman or under-assistant minority whip to exact tribute in the form of a payoff or campaign contribution. Every conference committee is a business opportunity for some legislator to see to it that certain desired changes are made in exchange for a favor or political deal. While spending limits and other financial controls may have their place, they are useless unless an effort is made to straighten out the twists and turns in the legislative route itself.

But the Founders didn't believe in legislative simplification. To the contrary, they believed in a path strewn with obstacles in the belief that it would encourage the kind of slow, deliberate politics that were their ideal. Instead, it has led to a level of legalized corruption unmatched since Georgian England. While the United States is hardly the only country with a bicameral legislature, it is the only one in which the two chambers are roughly equal in terms of political clout. It is the only one with a presidency that is also roughly equal and a judiciary that is equal as well. Moreover, it is only country mad enough to replicate this four-headed structure in forty-nine of the fifty states (Nebraska is the only state with a unicameral legislature), which are themselves on the same plane in many respects as the federal government.

Given such an impossibly complex structure, it is any wonder that the number of registered political lobbyists sets new records every year not only in Washington, but in the state capitals as well? Lobbyists buy and sell information and influence. Their stock in trade is their expertise in finding their way through the legislative or regulatory process. Each new regulation governing how much a donor can contribute and under what circumstances adds another layer of complexity, which in turn creates new demand for lobbyists' services. As long as structural reform is unthinkable, their numbers will continue to grow and the market in legislative services will continue to boom.

Rolling back the carceral state: One person-one vote means not only that every vote should count equally, but that every adult should be able to vote. Yet the United States has seen a winnowing of the voting rolls since the 1980s due to a combination of the War on Drugs, rising incarceration rates, and a little-noticed policy of disenfranchising felons and ex-felons. The result is a growing political subclass, overwhelmingly poor and nonwhite, that is deprived of political power at a time when it most needs to defend itself against the predations of the rich.

The scale of disenfranchisement is dramatic. As of December 2000, the number of Americans who had been deprived of the right to vote because they were currently or formerly in prison had reached an estimated 3.9 million, or one adult in fifty. Among black men, the number was 1.4 million, or one person in eight, while in seven states that permanently bar ex-offenders from voting, the proportion was one in four. All told, three out of ten black males in the next generation can expect to be disenfranchised at some point in their lives as a result of such policies.

This is the new Jim Crow, a form of racial purification whose consequences are already striking. In Florida, one of the states that permanently disenfranchises ex-felons, more than 400,000 people have been stricken from the rolls. Given that most ex-felons are poor, most would likely have voted Democratic in the 2000 presidential election. If even a small portion had gone to the polls, the result would have been a comfortable margin of victory for Gore in Florida and hence nationwide.

Only a portion of the voteless have been disenfranchised because they have been found guilty of violent crimes. By 1998, better than half of state and federal inmates, one million people in all, had been imprisoned for theft, drugs, and other nonviolent offenses, a figure better than three times that of the entire prison population of the European Union.[6] Yet, because they have been found guilty of felonies, most are deprived of their right to vote. From the point of view of the Republican oligarchy, policies like these not only victimize poor individuals, but have the added advantage of depriving the lower class in general of political clout so that the wealthy can exercise even greater sway. Democratic reform means taking aim at the War on Drugs, mass incarceration in general, and the mass disenfranchisement that goes with it.

Effective gun control: One person-one vote also means the ability to decide on all aspects of the political environment. Yet gun control is an area in which the people's impotence under the Constitution is all too apparent. The reason has to do with twenty-seven words of troublesome eighteenth-century prose known as the Second Amendment. "A well regulated Militia, being necessary to the security of a free State," it declares, "the right of the people to keep and bear Arms, shall not be infringed." After insisting for decades that the amendment guaranteed nothing more than the right to join the National Guard, the successor to the old militias, liberal constitutionalists since the late 1980s have done an about-face. One by one, they have come round to the point of view that the amendment does indeed guarantee a right of private gun ownership, although a few such as Laurence Tribe and Akhil Reed Amar continue to insist that such a right does not necessarily bar the door to more stringent forms of gun control.[7]

They are mistaken, however. If the Second Amendment protects an individual's right to bear arms, as the best scholarship now recognizes, then two things are evident: (1) the amendment's protection is in fact more emphatic than the First Amendment's comparatively oblique protection of free expression; and (2) while not ruling out gun control altogether (just as the First Amendment does not rule out regulation of free speech), it creates a presumption that regulation must not substantially limit a right that the amendment describes as nothing less than the cornerstone of a free republic. Gun control as the rest of the world understands it is therefore impossible.

This is more than just absurd. With opinion polls consistently showing between sixty and seventy percent of Americans favoring stepped-up gun control, it is potentially explosive. Rather than an obstacle to avoid, the Second Amendment is something that a democratic movement should tackle head on. Challenging it is a way not only of challenging the NRA, but of challenging an overly complicated amending clause that makes repeal all but impossible. Considering that the Second Amendment is part of the Bill of

Rights, it is a way of dispelling the religious aura that surrounds this particular document as well. After all, what better way is there to demonstrate the people's power than by changing the unchangeable?

Reining in war powers: American imperialism and an out-of-control American presidency are also the result of a growing crisis of democracy. The US denial of *popular* sovereignty has led to hypertrophied form of *national* sovereignty that is increasingly at war with the sovereignty of others. If democracy in the modern era has burst its national bounds and become increasingly internationalist, then American constitutionalism has also burst its national bounds and become increasingly super-nationalist. The "American Way," composed of equal parts limited government, the rule of law as opposed to the rule of the people, and an entirely self-serving conception of human rights and free trade, has become something that the United States is more and more determined to impose on others. Instead of drawing back in the wake of the Soviet collapse of 1989–91, as many liberals and social democrats had predicted, this "export strategy" has grown many times more aggressive. Democratization of American foreign policy not only means making it more accountable to the people of the United States, but more accountable to the people of the world. Certainly, congressional control over presidential war powers is one place to start.

Toward a Constitutional Convention? Although it is often assumed that this would be a way of wiping the slate clean and starting anew, the truth is otherwise. The problem with a Constitutional Convention is the method by which it would be called. Article V stipulates that Congress must call a convention "on the Application of the Legislatures of two thirds of the several States," adding that three-fourths of the states must then approve its recommendations before any of them become part of settled constitutional law. The upshot is a strongly state-centered process in which voting inside the convention would likely be state-by-state as well, just as it was in Philadelphia in 1787.

Could anything be more undemocratic? A convention formed under such auspices would be an attempt to reinvigorate states' rights in such a way as to bury one person-one vote for good. Rural whites in under-populated states from Alaska to Vermont would wield disproportionate power, while city dwellers and suburbanites from California, New York, and the other mega-states would wield less. One can only imagine the reactionary elements that would thrive in such a hothouse environment, the suburban tax rebels, Second Amendment gun nuts, neo-Confederates, and so on, all dedicated to the proposition that returning government to the people means returning it to its eighteenth-century roots. Those interested in modern democratic reform would find themselves shut out.

It's true that a Constitutional Convention could conceivably provide a window of opportunity for a neo-Jacobin party to take the podium and demand immediate national elections. But such a demand would succeed only to the degree that it was seen as clearly in favor of something new. Only a convention organized on democratic principles can further democracy.

WHAT IS NEEDED TO GET a modern democratic process underway? Mass political mobilization, obviously. But one thing we know from history is that political mobilization is impossible without an intellectual mobilization to clear the way. The French Revolution would not have taken place if the *philosophes* had not laid waste to the concept of aristocratic privilege, the civil rights revolution of the 1950s and '60s would never have happened if innumerable writers, journalists, and others had not taken similar aim at an entire body of racist ideology, and so forth. Any movement to dethrone the Constitution requires a comparable intellectual effort, one that is both radical and comprehensive, taking aim not merely at this or that feature, but at the central ideas on which the entire political structure rests. Understandably, historians and other political analysts have concentrated their attention on all the ways the United States has changed since its inception. Yet what seems more pressing after all these years is to point out all the ways it has remained the same. As far and away the oldest constitutional system on earth, the US is a relic of a pre-industrial era that has somehow survived into the modern world. True, its judges do not wear horsehair wigs and the Speaker of the House does not go about in old-fashioned, silver-buckle shoes and a black silk gown. None the less, its pre-modern origins are all too evident in the fetish it makes of checks and balances, in its superstitious fear of centralized political power, and in the absurd filiopietism it shows to the Founding Fathers. It is the most intensely conservative society in the advanced industrial world, one committed to the belief that the way to maintain freedom is to turn one's back on the modern world and devote oneself resolutely to the past. Rather than laboring to separate the wheat from the chaff, the more progressive aspects from the more regressive, a modern democratic movement must point out that the American constitutional tradition as a whole is exhausted and, as such, can only be a source for ideas whose implications are increasingly authoritarian. Any idea arising out of such a tradition must be presumed guilty unless proven innocent. Rather than from within, the only way to revitalize such a system is from without by tapping into international currents of socialism and democracy that are expressly opposed to American principles and methodologies.

Faith in a special American mission has been one of the few things that has united New Englanders and Virginians, Federalists and Anti-Federalists, liberals and conservatives. At its best, it has reflected the unshakable conviction of Puritans and abolitionists to overthrow kings, bishops, and planters and establish a true Christian commonwealth here on earth. At its worst, it is yet another example of hypocritical cant in the service of imperial adventures abroad or repression at home. It was one thing for Harriet Beecher Stowe, daughter of one Connecticut clergyman, wife of another, and author along the way of *Uncle Tom's Cabin*, to observe that Americans have been

> commissioned to bear the light of liberty and religion through all the earth and to bring in the great millennial day, when wars should cease and the whole world, released from the thralldom of evil, shall rejoice in the light of the Lord.[8]

But it was quite another for Woodrow Wilson to declare on the occasion of America's entry into World War I: "We have come to redeem the world by giving it liberty and justice." When a leading American scholar offered yet another encomium to the glorious wisdom of America's Founders in the mid-1960s, she was engaging in the sort of self-serving tautology that empires always engage in:

> [T]hese leading representatives of the American Enlightenment were a cluster of extraordinary men such as is rarely encountered in modern history. ... [N]either the Encyclopédie nor the salons, neither Socialists, liberal reformers, nor democrats and fanatical radicals who would come to brief power in the Jacobin and post-Jacobin phase of the [French] Revolution, produced statesmen capable of devising durable forms of government and exercising responsible power.[9]

America was so powerful in the mid-'60s, in other words, because its Founders were so far-seeing, while the Europeans had still not fully recovered from the war because its founders (written, needless to say, in lower case) were not. American power was proof of its greatness, while its greatness was the reason for its power.

Thirty or forty years later, with America heading off in an increasingly undemocratic direction, mental habits like these have degenerated into little more than a nervous tic on the part of a political culture that has given up on even the possibility of rational political analysis and structural reform. Al Gore was engaging in no more than the usual patriotic cant when he declared at the Democratic National Convention in August 2000:

> Yes, we have our problems. But the United States of America is the best country ever created and still, as ever, the hope of mankind. ... Yes, we're all imperfect. But as Americans we share in the privilege and challenge of building a more perfect union. ... If we allow ourselves to believe, without reservation, that we can do what's right and be the better for it, then the best America will become our America.[10]

Yet the goal must be to create a new political framework in which it is impossible for a politician to utter such nonsense without his audience erupting in wave after wave of derisive laughter.

It is not quite accurate to say that Americans have led the unexamined life. To the contrary, self-examination and even self-laceration have been common American themes. But as one might expect of a fundamentally Protestant culture, the self-laceration that Americans have engaged in from time to time has been of the Old Testament sort, the kind that occurs when a chosen people punishes itself for failing to live up to God's trust. What Americans have never done, on the other hand, is to take concepts like that of a chosen people or divine trust themselves and subject them to merciless examination. They have never tried to dethrone the concept of divinity and have thus ended up reinforcing it instead. The so-called American Enlightenment of the eighteenth-century was a pallid affair designed to place religion on a firmer intellectual footing. Yet what America needs is a real enlightenment whose goal is to drive out faith rather than replace it with some other form.

In the absence of such a movement, the outlook is grim. "We've all learned something about our government and Constitution," one senator said of the year 2000 election fiasco. "They are more fragile than we might have imagined."[11] As a result, the official response among both Democrats and Republicans has been to tiptoe ever more lightly in hope that the delicate structure is never again put to the test. What this means was evident from a front-page commentary that R.W. Apple, the *New York Times*'s senior Washington correspondent, wrote in January 2001 in response to lingering hard feelings over the Republican putsch:

> But the debate is likely to grow softer as the nation grows accustomed to pictures of Mr. Bush speaking from the Oval Office, boarding Air Force One, accompanied everywhere he goes by the strains of "Ruffles and Flourishes" and "Hail to the Chief." In the television age, those images, more than anything else, confer the mantle of authority and legitimacy on a leader.[12]

What is this but the fervent hope that the appearance of democratic legitimacy will soon crowd out the reality of electoral fraud, racial intimidation, and bullyboy tactics? In order to be made safe, American politics must be drained of what little substance they have left. If so, economic polarization will accelerate, the right-wing offensive will intensify, and America will grow ever more contemptuous of world opinion—which is precisely what the world has seen in the first few months of the Bush administration. The old doctrine of American Exceptionalism will be vindicated, but in a backhanded fashion. Where America seemed exceptionally prosperous and stable during the Cold War, it is now showing itself to be exceptionally undemocratic, exceptionally frozen in terms of its political development, and exceptionally punitive in terms of its social policies. If America were an obscure country in some far corner of the globe, it would be one thing. But it's the global hegemon, which means that its problem is simultaneously the world's.

NOTES

1 THE COLLAPSE

1 David Von Drehle, "The Night That Would Not End," *Washington Post*, November 9, 2000, p. A1; Kevin Sack and Frank Bruni, "How Gore Stopped Short On His Way to Concede," *New York Times*, November 9, 2000, p. A1.

2 Dan Keating, "Statistical Analysis Would Cheer Gore," *Washington Post*, December 5, 2000, p. A24.

3 R.W. Apple Jr., "Nation's Fault Line Divides Justices, Too," *New York Times*, December 10, 2000, p. A1.

4 Max Frankel, "Our System Leaves the Loser Standing," *New York Times*, December 15, 2000, p. A39.

5 Brian Whitaker, "Many countries are enjoying the U.S. shambles," *Guardian* (London), November 11, 2000, *Guardian* home pages, p. 3.

6 Paul Leicester Ford (ed.), *The Works of Thomas Jefferson* (New York: Putnam, 1905), vol. 12, p. 11.

7 Richard L. Berke, "Bush Prevails," *New York Times*, December 13, 2000, p. A1.

8 William M. Beaney, professor of constitutional law at the University of Denver, quoted in Dirk Johnson, "A 2d Election Day, and This One Counts," *New York Times*, December 15, 1992, p. B12.

9 White House Press Release, "Discussion Remarks in Town Hall Meeting on One America," December 3, 1997.

10 Edmund Burke, *Reflections on the Revolution in France* (London: Penguin Classics, 1986), pp. 194–5.

2 CONCEPTION

1 Catherine Drinker Bowen, *Miracle at Philadelphia: The Story of the Constitutional Convention, May to September, 1787* (Boston: Little, Brown, 1966).

2 Lord Bolingbroke, "The Idea of the Patriot King," in *Works* (Philadelphia: Cavey and Hart, 1841), vol. 2, p. 389.

3 See Joel Hurstfield, "Was There a Tudor Despotism After All?" *Transactions of the Royal Historical Society*, Fifth Series, vol. 17 (1967), for a thorough thrashing out of the issue.

4 Wallace T. MacCaffrey, "Parliament: The Elizabethan Experience," in Delloyd J. Guth and John W. McKenna (eds), *Tudor Rule and Revolution* (Cambridge: Cambridge University Press, 1982), p. 133.

5 Lewis Namier, *England in the Age of the American Revolution*, 2nd edn (London: Macmillan, 1961), p. 7.

6 Jack P. Greene, Introduction, *The American Revolution: Its Character and Limits* (New York: New York University Press, 1987), p. 8.

7 Alison Gilbert Olson, "Parliament, Empire, and Parliamentary Law, 1776," in J.G.A. Pocock, *Three British Revolutions: 1641, 1688, 1776* (Princeton: Princeton University Press, 1980), p. 309.

8 Don E. Fehrenbacher, *The Dred Scott Case: Its Significance in American Law and Politics* (New York: Oxford University Press, 1978), p. 211.

9 David Hackett Fischer, *Albion's Seed: Four British Folkways in America* (Oxford: Oxford University Press, 1989), p. 13.

10 Ibid., p. 257.

11 J.G.A. Pocock, *The Machiavellian Moment: Florentine Political Thought and the Atlantic Republican Tradition* (Cambridge: Cambridge University Press, 1957), p. 477.

12 John Brewer, *The Sinews of Power: War, Money, and the English State, 1688–1783* (London: Unwin Hyman, 1989), pp. 156–7.

13 Drew R. McCoy, *The Elusive Republic: Political Economy in Jeffersonian America* (New York: W.W. Norton, 1980), p. 61n.

14 Bernard Bailyn, *The Origin of American Politics* (New York: Knopf, 1968), pp. 40–1.

15 Quoted in Isaac Kramnick, *Bolingbroke and His Circle: The Politics of Nostalgia in the Age of Walpole* (Cambridge, Mass.: Harvard University Press, 1968), p. 251.

16 Bailyn, *Origin of American Politics*, p. 54.

17 Kramnick, *Bolingbroke and His Circle*, p. 262.

18 Montesquieu's friend and sponsor, Lord Chesterfield, later joined forces with Bolingbroke in the 1730s. See Franz Neumann, Introduction, Baron de Montesquieu, *The Spirit of the Laws* (New York: Macmillan, 1949), p. xii; also Basil Williams, *The Whig Supremacy, 1714–1760* (Oxford: Oxford University Press, 1962), pp. 203–4.

19 Jack P. Greene, "The Seven Years' War and the American Revolution," in Peter Marshall and Glyn Williams (eds), *The British Atlantic Empire Before the American Revolution* (London: Frank Cass, 1980), p. 87.

20 Samuel P. Huntington, *Political Order in Changing Societies* (New Haven: Yale University Press, 1968), pp. 106–8.

21 G.D.H. Cole and Raymond Postgate, *The Common People, 1746–1946* (London: Methuen, 1971), pp. 96–7; Derek Jarrett, *Britain 1688–1815* (London: Longmans, 1965), p 301.

22 Quoted in Hannah Arendt, *On Revolution* (London: Penguin, 1990), p. 62.

3   BIRTH

1 Willard Sterne Randall, *Thomas Jefferson: A Life* (New York: Henry Holt, 1993), p. 340.

2 Colin Bonwick, *The American Revolution* (Charlottesville: University Press of Virginia, 1991), pp. 127–31.

3 Thomas Jefferson, *Notes on the State of Virginia*, ed. William Peden (Chapel Hill: University of North Carolina Press, 1982), p. 120.

4   James Madison, *Notes of Debates in the Federal Convention of 1787*, ed. Adrienne Koch (New York: W.W. Norton, 1969), pp. 194–5. Madison's abbreviations, spellings, etc. have been updated in the interests of readability.

5   Ibid., pp. 251, 268.

6   Ibid., p. 240.

7   Ibid., p. 70.

8   Ibid., p. 406.

9   Ibid., pp. 80, 89.

10 Ibid., p. 42.

11 Ibid., p. 133.

12 Alexander Hamilton, James Madison, and John Jay, *The Federalist Papers* (New York: New American Library, 1961), p. 465.

13 Isaac Kramnick, *Republicanism and Bourgeois Radicalism: Political Ideology in Late Eighteenth-Century England and America*, (Ithaca, NY: Cornell University Press, 1990), p. 263.

14 Thomas Hobbes, *Leviathan* (Indianapolis: Bobbs-Merrill, 1958), p. 142.

15 Ibid.

16 Glenn Burgess, *The Politics of the Ancient Constitution: An Introduction to English Political Thought, 1603–1642* (University Park: Pennsylvania State University Press, 1992), p. 73.

17 Henry Adams, *The Great Secession Winter of 1860–61 and Other Essays* (New York: Sagamore, 1958), p. 194.

18 Hamilton, Madison, and Jay, *The Federalist Papers*, p. 106.

19 Madison, *Notes of Debates*, pp. 129–39.

20 Quoted in Seymour Martin Lipset, *Continental Divide: The Values and Institutions of the United States and Canada* (New York: Routledge, 1990), p. 206.

21 Charles Sellers, *The Market Revolution: Jacksonian America 1815–1846* (New York: Oxford University Press, 1991), p. 77.

22 Hamilton, Madison, and Jay, *The Federalist Papers*, p. 301.

23 John C. Miller, *The Federalist Era, 1789–1801* (New York: Harper & Row, 1960), p. 242.

4   VICTORY THROUGH FAILURE

1 Bertrand Russell, *A History of Western Philosophy* (New York: Simon and Schuster, 1945), p. 36.

2 Henry Adams, *History of the United States of America During the Administrations of Thomas Jefferson* (New York: Library of America, 1986), p. 108.

3 Todd S. Purdum, "Facets of Clinton," *New York Times Magazine*, May 19, 1996, p. 36.

4 Hamilton, Madison, and Jay, *The Federalist Papers*, p. 84.

5 Louis Hacker, *The Triumph of Capitalism in America* (New York: Simon and Schuster, 1940), p. 348.

6 Henry Steele Commager (ed.), *Documents of American History* (New York: Meredith, 1968), vol. 1, p. 428.

7 Bruce Ackerman, *We the People* (Cambridge, Mass.: Harvard University Press, 1991), vol. 1, p. 93.

8 Hans L. Trefousse, *Impeachment of a President: Andrew Johnson, the Blacks, and Reconstruction* (Knoxville: University of Tennessee Press, 1975), p. 178.

9 Michael Mann, *The Sources of Social Power* (Cambridge: Cambridge University Press, 1993), vol. 2, p. 635.

10 Sven Beckert, *The Monied Metropolis: New York City and the Consolidation of the American Bourgeoisie, 1850–1896* (Cambridge: Cambridge University Press, 2001), p. 297.

11 Stephen M. Griffin, "Constitutionalism in the United States," in Sanford Levinson (ed.), *Responding to Imperfection: The Theory and Practice of Constitutional Amendment* (Princeton: Princeton University Press, 1995), p. 47.

12 George E. Mowry, *The California Progressives* (Berkeley: University of California Press, 1951), pp. 50–1; Robert L. Heilbroner and Aaron Singer, *The Economic Transformation of America: 1600 to the Present* (San Diego: Harcourt Brace Jovanovich, 1984), p. 234; Gabriel Kolko, *The Triumph of Conservatism: A Reinterpretation of American History, 1900–1910* (New York: Free Press, 1963), pp. 163–4.

13 Merrill D. Peterson, *The Jefferson Image in the American Mind* (New York: Oxford University Press, 1962), p. 257.

14 "Mr. Ford's Page," *Dearborn Independent*, June 7, 1924, p. 7.

15 Burgess, *Politics of the Ancient Constitution*, p. 14.

16 The literature on Roosevelt's Jeffersonian beliefs and his anti-urban, pro-motorization policies is ample. See Daniel R. Fusfeld, *The Economic Thought of Franklin D. Roosevelt and the Origins of the New Deal* (New York: Columbia University Press, 1956); Joseph L. Arnold, *The New Deal in the Suburbs: A History of the Greenbelt Town Program, 1935–1954* (Columbus: Ohio State University Press, 1971); Reynold M. Wik, *Henry Ford and Grass-Roots America* (Ann Arbor: University of Michigan Press, 1972). See also Daniel Lazare, *America's Undeclared War: What's Killing Our Cities and How We Can Stop It* (New York: Harcourt, 2001), pp. 177–85.

17 Compare, for example, Lerner's criticism of both the Supreme Court and constitutional fetishism in his best-selling book, *It Is Later Than You Think: The Need for a Militant Democracy* (New York: Viking, 1938) with the constitutional piety of his study, *America as a Civilization: Life and Thought in the United States Today* (New York: Simon and Schuster, 1957).

18 Hamilton, Madison, and Jay, *The Federalist Papers*, pp. 465–6.

19 Anthony Chase, *Law and History: How American Legal Rules Change Over Time* (New York: New Press, 1997), p. 68.

20 Louis Hartz, *The Liberal Tradition in America: An Interpretation of American Political Thought Since the Revolution* (San Diego: Harcourt Brace Jovanovich, 1983), p. 50.

21 Richard Harwood and Haynes Johnson, "A Solemn Change," *Washington Post*, August 9, 1974, p. 1.

5 THE LONG GOODBYE

1 "Excerpts From Debate on Plan to Begin Impeachment Inquiry," *New York Times*, October 9, 1998, pp. A23–4.

2 Raoul Berger, *Impeachment: The Constitutional Problems* (Cambridge, Mass.: Harvard University Press, 1973), pp. 19–62.

3 Gwen Ifill, "President Chooses Breyer, An Appeals Judge in Boston, for Blackmun's Seat," *New York Times*, May 14, 1994, p. A1.

4 Telephone interview, Marc Maurer, executive director, The Sentencing Project, Washington, DC, February 13, 2001; The Center on Juvenile and Criminal Justice/Justice Policy Institute, "Too Little Too Late: President Clinton's Prison Legacy," available at www.cjcj.org; Human Rights Watch, *Punishment and Prejudice: Racial Disparities in the War on Drugs* (New York, May 2000), pp. 10, 17, 19; Patricia Allard and Marc Mauer, *Regaining the Vote: An Assessment of Activity Relating to Felon Disenfranchisement Laws* (Washington, DC: The Sentencing Project, January 2000).

5 Up-to-date information on American capital punishment is available from the Death Penalty Information Center at www.deathpenaltyinfo.org

6 Don Lattin, "WWJD? Once only the religious right asked that question," *San Francisco Chronicle*, September 15, 2000, p. A1.

7 Ceci Connolly, "Lieberman Urges 'Place for Faith in Our Public Life,'" *Washington Post*, August 28, 2000, p. A1.

8 Michael Hardt and Antonio Negri, *Empire* (Cambridge, Mass.: Harvard University Press, 2000), p 163.

9 Although flawed in important respects, Robert Brenner's recent discussion of the downturn in the capitalist long wave is the most comprehensive to date. See Robert Brenner, "The Economics of Global Turbulence," *New Left Review* I/229 (May–June 1998).

10 Theodore J. Lowi, *The Personal President: Power Invested, Promise Unfulfilled* (Ithaca: Cornell University Press, 1985), pp. 68–9.

11 Morris P. Fiorina, *Divided Government* (New York: Macmillan, 1992), pp. 7, 65–6.

12 Katharine Q. Seelye, "Files Show How Gingrich Laid a Grand G.O.P. Plan," *New York Times*, December 3, 1995, p. 1.

13 For an unsparing analysis of the liberal collapse, see Theodore J. Lowi,

The End of Liberalism: The Second Republic of the United States (New York: W.W. Norton, 1979).

14 James T. Patterson, *Grand Expectations: The United States, 1945–1974* (New York: Oxford University Press, 1996), p. 437.

15 "From a republican standpoint, as classically understood—with a small 'r' —the summary removal of any President would be desirable, as a lesson to all others." Perry Anderson, "Testing Formula Two," *New Left Review* 8 (March/April 2001), p. 14.

16 "Exchanges Between the Candidates in the Third Presidential Debate," *New York Times*, October 18, 2000, p. A26.

17 Evelyn Nieves, "A Party Crasher's Lone Regret: That He Didn't Get More Votes," *New York Times*, February 18, 2001, sec. 4, p. 1.

18 Toby Eckert, "As tight race enters homestretch, Gore steps up pace, Bush cruises," *San Diego Union-Tribune*, November 2, 2000, p. A1.

19 Dan Balz, "Gore, Bush Hit Illinois And Other Key States," *Washington Post*, November 3, 2000, p. A1.

20 Gary M. Halter, *Government and Politics of Texas: A Comparative View* (New York: McGraw-Hill, 1999), pp. 132–58.

21 Chandler Davidson, *Race and Class in Texas Politics* (Princeton: Princeton University Press, 1990), pp. 79, 84; Beryl E. Pettus and Randall W. Bland, *Texas Government Today: Structure, Functions, Political Processes* (Homewood, Ill.: Dorsey Press, 1984), p. 245. See also Daniel Lazare, "Le modèle texan menace les Etats-Unis," *Le Monde diplomatique*, September 2000, pp. 12–13. English translation available at www.en.monde-diplomatique.fr/2000/09/14texas.

22 "Election Snafus Went Far Beyond Florida In Year When It Mattered," *Wall Street Journal*, November 17, 2000, p. A1; Bryan Gruley and Chip Cumins, "Election Day Became A Nightmare, as Usual, For Bernalillo County," *Wall Street Journal*, December 15, 2000, p. A1; Gary Fields and Jennifer Davit, "In Selma, a Landmark Of Civil Rights, Voting Can Still Be a Struggle," *Wall Street Journal*, December 18, 2000, p. A1.

23 Gary Wills, "The Making of the President, 2000," *New York Times*, April 1, 2001, sec. 7, p. 8.

24 The Washington Post Company, *Deadlock: The Inside Story of America's Closest Election* (New York: Public Affairs, 2001), pp. 140–1.

25 Nicholas Kulish and Jim Vandehei, "Protest in Miami-Date a Well-Organized GOP Effort," *Wall Street Journal*, November 27, 2000, p. A40.

26 "A Gore Coup d'Etat?" *Wall Street Journal*, November 10, 2000, p. A18; William J. Bennett, "Gore Challenge Undermines U.S. Democracy," *Wall Street Journal*, November 13, 2000, p. A36; Paul A. Gigot, "Burgher Rebellion: GOP Turns Up Miami Heat," *Wall Street Journal*, November 24, 2000, p. A16.

27 Mackubin Thomas Owens, "The Democratic Party's War on the Military," *Wall Street Journal*, November 22, 2000, p. A22.

28 Katharine Q. Seelye, "Some Allies Urge Gore to Concede, but Most Democrats Wait for His Move," *New York Times*, December 13, 2000, p. A23.

29 "In His Remarks, Gore Says He Will Help Bush 'Bring Americans Together,'" *New York Times*, December 14, 2000, p. A26.

30 George H. Sabine, *A History of Political Theory*, 3rd edn (London: George G. Harrap, 1963), p. 202.

31 See E.J. Hobsbawm, *The Age of Revolution: 1789–1848* (New York: New American Library, 1962), esp. pp. 77–80.

32 The Washington Post Company, *Deadlock*, p. 83.

33 Dean E. Murphy, "In Upstate Victory Tour, Mrs. Clinton Says Electoral College Should Go," *New York Times*, November 11, 2000, p. B1.

34 Ronald Dworkin, "A Badly Flawed Election," *New York Review of Books*, January 11, 2001, p. 55.

35 Robert Kuttner, "Democrats Make Nice While Bush Runs Hard Right," *American Prospect Online*, January 8, 2001, available at www.prospect.org.

6   IS THERE A WAY OUT?

1 Editorial, "The Case for the Electoral College," *New York Times*, December 19, 2000, p. A34.

2 Sanford Levinson, "How Many Times Has the United States Constitution Been Amended? (A) <26; (B) 26; (C) 27; (D) >27," in Sanford Levinson (ed.), *Responding to Imperfection: The Theory and Practice of Constitutional Amendment* (Princeton: Princeton University Press, 1995), pp. 13–36.

3 Jeffrey H. Birnbaum, "The Man Who Could Be President," *Fortune*, March 29, 1999, p. 72.

4 Latest census figures are available at www.census.gov.

5 Frances E. Lee and Bruce I. Oppenheimer, *Sizing Up the Senate: The Unequal Consequences of Equal Representation* (Chicago: University of Chicago Press, 1999), pp. 10–11.

6 Vincent Schiraldi, Jason Ziedenberg, and John Irwin, "America's One Million Nonviolent Prisoners" (Washington, DC: The Justice Policy Institute, 1999), available at www.cjcj.org.

7 See Sanford Levinson, "The Embarrassing Second Amendment," *Yale Law Journal* 99 (December 1989); Joyce Lee Malcolm, *To Keep and Bear Arms: The Origins of an Anglo-American Right* (Cambridge, Mass.: Harvard University Press, 1994); Laurence H. Tribe and Akhil Reed Amar, "Well-Regulated Militias, and More," *New York Times*, October 28, 1999. See also Daniel Lazare, "Your Constitution Is Killing You," *Harper's*, October 1999.

8 Robert N. Bellah, *et al.*, *The Good Society* (New York: Knopf, 1991), p. 35.

9 Adrienne Koch, *The American Enlightenment: The Shaping of An American Experiment and a Free Society* (New York: George Braziller, 1965), pp. 35, 39–40.

10 "Gore to Delegates and Nation: 'My Focus Will Be on Working Families'," *New York Times*, August 18, 2000, pp. A21–22.

11 New Jersey Democrat Robert Torricelli, quoted in Richard L. Berke, "Bush Prevails," *New York Times*, December 13, 2000, p. A1.

12 R.W. Apple Jr., "Tradition and Legitimacy," *New York Times*, January 21, 2001, p. A1.

INDEX